How to Invest
in the
UK Property
Market

If you want to know how. . .

Investing in Student Buy-to-Let
How to make money from student accommodation

The Self-Build Survival Guide
How to survive building or renovating your dream home –
the eco-friendly way

How to Buy a Flat
All you need to know on apartment living and letting

The New Landlord's Guide to Letting
How to buy and let residential property for profit

Getting the Builders In
A step-by-step guide to supervising your own building projects

howtobooks

Send for a free copy of the latest catalogue to:

How To Books
Spring Hill House, Spring Hill Road,
Begbroke, Oxford OX5 1RX. United Kingdom.
info@howtobooks.co.uk
www.howtobooks.co.uk

How to Invest
in the
UK Property
Market

Gerry FitzGerald

howtobooks

Published by How To Books Ltd,
Spring Hill House, Spring Hill Road,
Begbroke, Oxford OX5 1RX. United Kingdom.
Tel: (01865) 375794. Fax: (01865) 379162.
info@howtobooks.co.uk
www.howtobooks.co.uk

How To Books greatly reduce the carbon footprint of their books by sourcing their typesetting and printing in the UK.

British Library Cataloguing in Publication Data
A catalogue record for this book is available from the British Library

ISBN 978 1 84528 244 8

Produced for How To Books by Deer Park Productions, Tavistock, Devon
Typeset by PDQ Typesetting, Newcastle-under-Lyme, Staffs
Printed and bound by Bell & Bain Ltd, Glasgow

NOTE: The material contained in this book is set out in good faith for general guidance and no liability can be accepted for loss or expense incurred as a result of relying in particular circumstances on statements made in the book. The laws and regulations are complex and liable to change, and readers should check the current position with the relevant authorities before making personal arrangements.

Solely for convenience, the terms 'he', 'him' and 'his' have been used throughout this work. They should be understood to include 'she' and 'her'.

Contents

Preface

Suppose you have £15,000 to spare and you decide to invest this sum in the stock market. You hear about a scheme which allows you to buy £100,000 worth of shares for a personal outlay of just £15,000. The other £85,000 you can borrow, using the shares as collateral. Most or all of the cost of this borrowing will be met by somebody else. At the same time the shares (which have in reality only cost you £15,000) remain yours and you will benefit from any capital growth in the future!

Of course, no such scheme exits for any form of stock market investment. But it does for property.

Banks and building societies are the source of the loan while your tenants help to repay it for you. Getting this formula to work isn't always easy and decisions have to be made with great care. But the blueprint is there and it exits *uniquely* for the property market.

Consider the alternatives:

PROPERTY AND EQUITIES

For most people access to equities is though shares, unit trusts (pooled investments) and their ugly sister, OEICs (open-ended investment contracts).

We are all aware, when making such an investment, that values can fall as well as rise and that stock market investment should be for the medium to long term. Any dividend or income can also fluctuate. It took the dotcom catastrophe, however, to remind us that values can fall to near extinction and dividend income disappear into a black hole.

Property, of course, is not immune to market fluctuations and a severe fall in property values shook the market in the UK in the late 1980s. But at no point did property become entirely worthless as an investment. Although values remained depressed throughout this period, rental income continued to flow while rental demand increased considerably, boosting rents even further. While capital growth faltered, income remained robust and healthy.

TAX BREAKS FOR EQUITIES

To encourage us to save, the government offers a number of tax goodies, both for long-term savings (pensions) and medium-term savings (PEPs and ISAs).

Pensions

By far the most important of these is pensions. State funding for retirement has always been pitifully low in the UK. Instead, the government prefers to encourage us to make our own provision, offering tax incentives to do so.

In the case of pensions, there is tax relief at one's marginal rate on the pension contribution, while on retirement 25% of the fund can be taken as a tax-free lump sum. How does this compare with property investment?

There is no denying the tax advantages of pension planning. For a 40% taxpayer, a £100 p.m. contribution, in effect, costs just £60. A quarter of the fund can be taken in cash, on retirement, and this too is tax free. At the same time any growth in the pension fund is, for the most part, free of tax. While property investment can't match these tax breaks (although we shall see that tax relief in some measure is available), it surpasses pension planning in three fundamental ways:

◆ Only 25% of the pension fund can normally be accessed in cash as a lump sum (and then not before the age of 50, rising to 55 in 2010). The rest of the fund is used by the insurance company to provide the annual pension. It effectively disappears, never to be seen again (the only exception being where the pensioner dies before 75). A property does not disappear at any stage of the investment and can be realised for its full cash value at any time. The investor always retains full ownership of the asset.

◆ While tax relief reduces the real cost of a pension contribution, the bulk of the pension premium must still be paid by the investor. It is the tenant, however, not the property investor, who makes the bulk of the payments needed to purchase the property.

◆ Contributions to a pension are strictly limited on an annual and a lifetime basis, with an overall cap placed on the value of the resulting pension pot. There are no restrictions on property investment or the value of a property portfolio.

It should also be remembered that tax breaks are subject to the whim of the Chancellor and can be withdrawn at any time. It is known, for example, that successive Chancellors have had their eye on the tax-free lump sum and have questioned, more than once, the generosity of the 40% tax relief on contributions for the better-off. If anyone thinks this wouldn't happen, consider this: there was a time when pension fund managers were able to reclaim tax paid on dividend income. Not any more. At a stroke the Chancellor of the day withdrew this tax break and instantly grabbed £5 billion a year from pension funds. We have been warned!

PEPs and ISAs

Personal equity plans and individual savings accounts (which replaced them) are also intended to lure the investor into the stock market. Unlike pensions they are considerably more flexible, with access to the full fund at all times. The fund value, whenever it is taken, is free of tax. Unlike pensions, however, there is no tax relief on the contribution itself. There is also a strict limit (typically as low as £7,000) on the investment that can be made in any one tax year. As a savings vehicle for the medium term they are a useful complement to pension planning. The miserly annual limit on investment, however, severely restricts their long-term potential and, of course, nobody pays your contribution for you! PEPs and ISAs have nothing on property investment.

This is not, of course, to say that shares, pensions and ISAs do not have their place in a balanced portfolio of investments. But they are no longer the only, or best, show in town.

Gerry FitzGerald

Part One

The Concept

Supply and Demand

Property, like all markets, is governed by supply and demand.

It is almost a truism to say that the British, unlike their continental neighbours, are a nation of homeowners (and shopkeepers, as Napoleon observed). This fact alone has provided, and continues to provide, a powerful demand for house purchase. But house building has never kept pace with demand. Between 1990 and 2000 house building fell from 200,000 units per annum to 180,000, while the number of households grew by two million. London alone needs 35,000 new homes a year and has little prospect of getting them. It is hardly surprising, therefore, that there is an acute shortage of available property.

But while demand clearly outstrips supply in the case of house purchase, what about the *rental* market? Consider the following.

FIRST TIMERS

The first-time buyer is, surprisingly, a key player in the rental market. As the shortage of supply pushes prices up, outpacing increases in wages and salaries, the first-time buyer has had to wait longer and longer to get on the first rung of the housing ladder. The average age of the first-time buyer is now 35. What does he do in the meantime? He rents.

LATE DEVELOPERS

Decisions on careers, marriage and starting a family are now being made later in life than ever before, no doubt in part due to changes in the job market and the increased uptake of university places.

UNIVERSITIES

Thirty years ago 5% of sixth formers went on to university. Today the government is well placed to achieve its objective of 50%! In recent years expansion in tertiary education has been breathtaking, with universities competing furiously for the student market. This market, it is worth noting, is not solely UK based. Admissions departments send representatives overseas to attract foreign students (earning substantially more from them than from their UK counterparts). It is not unusual to find some post-graduate courses entirely filled by overseas students!

No amount of student accommodation on-campus can cope with this demand. Without the private rented sector, universities would be in serious crisis.

UNTIL DEATH US DO. . .

Not any more it seems. The divorce rate in this country has risen year on year over the last 20 years and is heading relentlessly towards 50%. Where there was one household before there is now a need for two. In many cases the second home is initially rented.

IMMIGRATION

The UK has always needed immigrants (there would be no roads without the Irish and no London Transport without West Indians). With the fall in the birth rate and the inevitable consequences of an ever growing elderly population (not enough young people in work to pay for retired people's pensions), the need for young immigrant workers is now greater than ever. With the expansion of the EU to 27 member states, workers from other countries, East Europeans in particular, are free to come here to fill the gap. They have to live somewhere.

ASYLUM SEEKERS

Unexpected immigrants cause a separate housing headache. The burden of providing homes for these families has fallen, in the main, to local councils. The solution, until recently, was bed-and-breakfast accommodation at enormous cost. Now there is a far cheaper and more satisfactory answer – private sector housing, rented directly to the council.

SOCIAL HOUSING

Apart from asylum seekers, councils are obliged to assist many others in their housing requirements. This can take the form of providing housing benefit for renting in the private sector or renting homes directly from landlords for the use of their clients.

THE JOB MARKET

The permanent job for life has long gone. In its place we have contract work, self-employment, employment agencies, temporary work. Flexibility and mobility are now essential requirements in the workplace. Few expect to stay in the same job and live in the same area indefinitely. Renting is the sensible option for many in this position.

While house purchase, therefore, remains a powerful long-term goal for most people, it is clear that there is and will always be a steady demand for rental accommodation.

$$\textbf{2}$$

The Risks

Yes, there are risks!

Despite the highly promising scenario outlined in the previous chapters, things can go wrong and undoubtedly will in the course of your investment. Here are some of the most likely.

PRICE FALLS

Nobody likes to think of house prices falling, particularly if there has been a sustained period of above-average rises and we have been lulled into believing it will always be like this. Unfortunately, however, prices do fall (and are more likely to do so after a sustained period of above-average rises). How does this affect the market?

With regards to the reduced value of a property portfolio, this should not worry the investor seriously. Property investment is for the *long term*. Prices can be expected to fluctuate. It is the long-term gain that matters. In addition, it is normally not possible to borrow more than 85% of the property's value, so the risk of negative equity (where you owe more than the property is worth) is slight. But what about the rental market?

When prices start to fall it might be expected that more people will decide to buy. This is not so. They decide to wait! Nobody, after all, wants to buy now when prices may have much further to fall. As a result, the decision to buy is put off. In the meantime, would-be purchasers rent.

While first-time buyers delay their purchase, so do many investors, and for the same reason. This, too, affects the rental market because fewer properties become available to let. There is, therefore, both a *reduced supply of* and *an increased demand for* rental accommodation. The net effect is to improve considerably the lot of the landlord. It is easier to find tenants and easier to review rents upwards when tenancy agreements are due for renewal.

PRICE RISES

Price rises are more serious problem for the rental market. The perception of ever increasing price rises attracts the wrong sort of investor – the short-term, capital gain speculator. The difficulty here is that, while the speculator is waiting for his capital gain, he lets his property. This has the effect of increasing the supply of rented accommodation and temporarily *depressing rents*.

The investor who has bought the right sort of property in the right area and with a view to the long term will not be greatly affected by this. Such an investor can wait for the market to turn. When prices reach their peak, the speculators will go and sanity will return. Unfortunately, as we shall see, the less careful investor could well suffer in the meantime.

INTEREST RATE RISES

We are all at the mercy of mortgage rate fluctuations. While the occasional quarter point rise will make little difference, a succession of such increases will hurt. But will they cause serious damage?

Buy-to-let lenders are a canny lot and have already thought of this. As we shall see, such mortgages are based on an independent estimate of the rental income. In addition, most prudent lenders insist that the rent should be 125% or 130% of the monthly mortgage cost. By protecting themselves in this way, mortgage lenders are also protecting their customers.

VOIDS

An ugly term to describe periods when a property is without tenants.

It is sensible to expect some periods during which a property will not be let. One month in 12 is a good rule of thumb. The simple way to deal with voids is to plan ahead and anticipate a rental income for no more than 11 months a year.

As for the property itself, there is the risk that if it is empty for a prolonged period of time it may attract squatters. It will need to be watched carefully. There is also the matter of building insurance. If the property is empty for more than a specified time (anywhere between one month and three), the insurer may not pay out in the event of a claim. Check the policy schedule and advise the insurer of any change of circumstances that might affect a claim.

Part Two

Finance

3

The Buy-to-Let Mortgage

There was a time when a mortgage to buy an investment residential property was virtually impossible. The problem was simply that lenders applied the same lending criteria to such transactions as they did to a normal residential mortgage. In other words, the commercial aspect of the venture (the rent) was ignored and the borrower was expected to fund the mortgage entirely from his *earned* income. If there was a mortgage already in place on another property, the earned income would have to be sufficient to cover both mortgages! Not surprisingly, there wasn't a great deal of scope for investing in the residential sector.

In the late 1990s, the buy-to-let (BTL) mortgage changed all that. Lenders decided, in effect, to ignore any existing mortgage and to concentrate instead on the new BTL purchase. What mattered was not the borrower's personal earned income but the potential *rental* income from the new investment.

To protect themselves (and the borrower) they set strict limits on the amount that could be borrowed and also required that the rent should comfortably exceed the interest paid on the mortgage. In the early days the maximum mortgage available was 75% of the purchase price. This gradually moved to 85% which is now the norm (although some lenders will offer 90%). The rent must be 125% or 130% (depending on the lender) of the mortgage interest payment. A few lenders, however, will take a more relaxed view and accept 110% or 115%. A few will even consider 100% if the borrowing level is very low.

An additional incentive for lenders was the new assured shorthold tenancy (AST) introduced by the Housing Act 1988. This *assured* the tenant the right to the property for the term of the tenancy (six or 12 months) but also, crucially, *assured* the landlord the right to recover possession easily and quickly at the end of the tenancy. The risk of being saddled with a tenant for life had disappeared (see Chapter 23).

4

The Let-to-Buy Mortgage

A little known but very useful product is the let-to-buy mortgage. This is designed for the investor who intends to let out his own home and buy another which will then become his main residence. If the lender is happy that the first property can be successfully let he may ignore the mortgage on that property and offer a let-to-buy mortgage for the new purchase.

THE LETTING

The underlying principle here is that the rent from letting the first property should cover the mortgage on that property, thus enabling the new lender to ignore it altogether when calculating the mortgage for the new purchase. Surprisingly, however, there is wide variation among lenders as to their requirements regarding the letting of the first property. You may encounter any of the following:

- No requirement for a separate rental assessment. The lender will settle for a letter from a local letting agent indicating the likely rent level. The borrower can arrange this.

- A requirement for a separate rental assessment to be arranged by the lender (using an independent valuer) and paid for by the borrower.

- The rent should be enough to cover the interest paid on the mortgage.

◆ The rent should exceed the mortgage interest by 25% or 30%.

◆ Where the mortgage is on a repayment basis, the rent should cover both capital and interest.

THE BUYING

If the lender is happy with the letting arrangements for the first property, the mortgage on the new purchase will be a normal residential mortgage, not linked in any way to the rental potential of that property. Crucially, however, *the cost of servicing the first mortgage will be ignored.*

The deposit for the new purchase is frequently raised by remortgaging the existing property with a new lender (often the lender providing the mortgage on the new property). If there is no change to the existing mortgage arrangements, the present lender must be notified that the property will no longer be owner occupied and will be let out. A lender can refuse permission for this or charge a higher interest rate when the property is let. It is often simpler to remortgage with the new lender.

5

100% Finance?

Buy-to-let (BTL) lenders will always require a deposit. This is usually 15%, with a few lenders accepting 10%. *There are no 100% BTL mortgages.* If you have no ready funds available, therefore, you will have to borrow the deposit. But how do you do this?

If you already have a residential mortgage on your own property and there is sufficient equity in the property (the difference between its value and the outstanding mortgage), you may be able to borrow additional funds from your existing lender. This is undoubtedly the quickest and the cheapest way to raise the cash you need. However, there are several hurdles to leap:

◆ First, your *earned* income must be sufficient to satisfy the lender that you can service the extra amount.

◆ Secondly, your lender will want to know what you want the extra cash for. Some residential lenders will not countenance borrowing for the purpose of raising the deposit for another purchase. They fear you may be getting in over your head.

◆ Thirdly, your lender will carry out a new credit check to make sure nothing has changed since your original mortgage was arranged. If your credit rating has changed for the worse (e.g. defaults on credit card payments or county court judgments), this could pose problems, not only making the extra borrowing impossible but also alerting your lender to your current financial problems.

If you don't already have a mortgaged property (i.e. you are a first-time buyer) and you have no cash available for a deposit, the problems you face are considerably greater. First, leaving aside the missing deposit, the vast majority of BTL lenders require you to have an existing residential mortgage before they will consider you for a BTL loan (see below). Secondly, the possible route to the elusive deposit in this case is slow and uncertain. This is what you need to do:

◆ First, buy a property for *your own use* on a 100% residential mortgage (100% mortgages, though rare, do exist for residential purchases).

◆ Secondly, the property you buy should be one that can be improved, thus increasing in value (typically requiring some or all of the following: new bathroom, kitchen, central heating, double glazing).

◆ Finally, remortgage with another lender to raise the cash on the new increased value of the property you have bought and improved.

Simple? Not as simple as it looks. Lenders will advance 100% (or even more) but on very stringent criteria. The borrower:

◆ must have an impeccable credit rating
◆ should be employed rather than self-employed
◆ should be well out of any probationary period
◆ should have good prospects of advancement

◆ should have a sufficiently high income to satisfy the lender's income requirements for a 100% mortgage.

As you can see, such loans are not available for everyone.

If the property you buy obviously needs improvement, it may well be possible to increase its value by carrying out the improvements. But how will you pay for this if you have no available cash? Moreover, the sort of improvements that can have a significant impact on the value are, by definition, expensive – new kitchen, new bathroom, central heating and double glazing.

Finally, if all these obstacles are overcome, a new mortgage needs to be raised on the property you have improved. Here you will encounter an unexpected problem – the loan-to-value ratio (LTV) applicable to remortgages. You may have had a 100% mortgage for the original purchase but few lenders will advance more than 90% on a remortgage and none will do 100%. Care needs to be taken that the projected 'new value' of the property will be sufficient to take this into account. Also, bear in mind that the new mortgage has built-in costs – valuation fees, legal costs, mortgage arrangement fees and possibly broker fees. These must also be budgeted for.

In practical terms, 100% finance for a BTL mortgage is possible only for the investor who has an existing residential mortgage. For the first-time buyer it is a pure myth.

6

Choosing a Lender

With the default rate of buy-to-let (BTL) mortgages lower than that of residential mortgages and with interest rates higher, the BTL market has proved a remarkable success story for lenders. As a result, competition for this business has increased greatly in recent years with more and more lenders offering a BTL product range. How do you choose between them?

MAINSTREAM OR SPECIALIST

For most high-street lenders, BTL is an add-on. Their core business remains residential mortgages for owner occupiers. For that reason, when it comes to BTL, they tend to be unduly restrictive in one way or another. For example, a lender may insist that some element of personal income, in addition to the rent, be taken into account when calculating the mortgage to be offered. Others may lend only to 80% or 75%. Some will limit to just a few the number of BTL properties you may purchase or put a cap on the total value of your portfolio. Few will help you if you have had any credit problems in the past. All will be considerably less generous in their calculation of the maximum mortgage you can have. For the serious investor the specialist lender remains the best choice.

FIRST-TIME BUYER

Most lenders will not offer a BTL mortgage to a first-time buyer. They expect you to have your own residential mortgage already. Only one or two will consider first-time buyers. It is vital to check this point with the lender, directly or through a broker, before embarking on a decision in principle request (see Chapter 10) or full application. You will not only be wasting your time but you will also leave too many footprints on your credit file (see Chapter 10).

INTEREST RATES

Surprisingly, the lowest rates are not generally best for the BTL investor, for they usually come with unacceptable conditions. A particularly low initial rate, for example, may tie the borrower in for a number of years *after* the rate has changed back to the higher variable rate. Changing to another lender during this 'extended tie-in' will incur a hefty penalty. In addition, as we shall see, choosing the lowest rate available always means sacrificing the maximum mortgage available. For most investors the priority is to borrow as much as possible.

CHARGES

These vary widely from lender to lender. All have an arrangement fee (which can be added to the loan), but this fee can range from a few hundred pounds to as much as 1.75% of the amount borrowed! Because it is added to the loan (few choose to pay it up front), there is a tendency to disregard it. It is, however, a very costly add-on as interest is also paid on this amount for the duration of the mortgage.

In addition to the arrangement fee (sometimes called a completion fee), some lenders charge a 'mortgage indemnity guarantee' fee, or MIG. This is essentially an insurance premium paid by the borrower, but for the sole benefit of the lender. If the lender repossesses the property but fails to recover the full mortgage amount on resale, the insurance company will pay the lender the difference (the insurance company can then legally pursue the hapless borrower to recover the sum it has paid out!).

MAXIMUM MORTGAGE

Most lenders agree that the rent should exceed the mortgage interest (*not* capital and interest) by a certain amount. But they differ on two important counts – the definition of 'interest' and the margin by which it should be exceeded.

For most lenders the 'interest' is not the rate you pay (which may be quite low initially) but the standard variable rate (much higher) charged by the lender. A few lenders, however, base the calculation on the pay rate. Since this will normally be lower than the variable rate, the mortgage available is correspondingly higher. In addition, some lenders require the rent to be 130%, others just 125% of the mortgage interest. A few will come down to 115% or 110%. Choosing a lender with the right formula is crucial if you want the maximum mortgage possible.

CASE STUDY

The following case studies are based on estimated rental income of £900 p.m. (£10,800 p.a.) and a purchase price of £177,000.

A mortgage of £150,450 (85%) is required. The lenders chosen will allow a maximum borrowing of 85% subject to the rent/interest calculation.

- Lender A requires the rent to be 130% of the interest. The interest is the variable rate of 6.5% rather than the rate you actually pay. The maximum mortgage on this basis is £127,810, based on the following calculation:

$$\frac{10,800 \times 100}{130} = 8307.69 \qquad \frac{8307.69 \times 100}{6.5} = 127,810.61$$

■ Lender B also requires the rent to be 130% of the interest but the interest rate is 5.74%, the rate you pay for the first three years. In this case the maximum mortgage is £144,733.

■ Lender C requires the rent to be 125% of the interest. The interest rate, again, is the 5.74% pay rate. In this case the maximum mortgage available is £150,522.

All three lenders will happily provide a BTL mortgage but only lender C will advance the full 85% of the purchase price – £150,450.

DRAWDOWN FACILITY

Specialist BTL lenders are aware that this may not be the only purchase the borrower will make. Some will accordingly offer a drawdown facility to help in future transactions.

The principle here is that the lender will advance up to a certain percentage (typically 85%) of the property value. If the property has increased in value since the purchase a lender who offers a drawdown facility will allow the borrower to drawdown (i.e. borrow further funds for a deposit on further property purchase, repairs, etc.). The only proviso is that the rent is sufficient to meet the lender's criteria for the advance (see above).

This has very significant benefits for the serious investor. For a start, there is no need to spend time and money on remortgaging with another lender. In a matter of days and with a minimum of fuss the funds are transferred to your bank account. If you are buying abroad or at auction and need to buy for cash, this facility is invaluable. Lenders who don't offer this arrangement should be avoided.

LIMITED COMPANY MORTGAGES

Few lenders will offer BTL mortgages to limited companies. Of those who do, most require that a new company be set up solely for this purpose (an SPV, or special purpose vehicle). Only a tiny number will allow an existing company to borrow.

PROPERTY RESTRICTIONS

When the BTL mortgage was first introduced, lenders were extremely cautious. Apart from restricting the maximum loan to 75% of the property value, they also refused to consider altogether certain property types. These were ex-local authority properties, studios and flats over commercial premises. The reasoning was quite simple. If the borrower defaulted, the lender would have to sell the property. Such properties were considered difficult to sell (ironically, tenants love them!).

Ex-local

Initially, both flats and houses were excluded. Now, however, houses are accepted by all lenders. In the case of flats, there is still a problem. This applies, in particular, to tall blocks of flats and to blocks of a certain construction. Most lenders will still not consider apartment blocks of more than five storeys, regardless of which floor the flat in question is on.

In the 1960s there was a popular method of construction for local authority apartment blocks involving an external cladding of concrete slabs, now considered unsafe. Blocks with this feature are still unacceptable to most lenders.

Studios
Once regarded as the Cinderella of the property world, studios are now widely accepted. They must, however, be large and in very good condition.

Over shops
This particular problem has eased but has not disappeared. Many lenders will not entertain a mortgage on an apartment over any kind of commercial premises. Those who do (just a few!) are very specific about exclusions. These are: no launderettes, no dry cleaners, no restaurants, no take-aways, no hair salons. The one thing in common with this list is *smell*. Chemicals and cooking odours do not appeal to potential buyers. BTL lenders won't touch them.

It follows from the above that, if the property you have your heart set on fits into this list of undesirables, you will have to be absolutely certain there is a lender out there who will accommodate you. It is also worth bearing in mind that you will, one day, want to sell this property and your potential buyer will face the same problems.

BUILDERS' INCENTIVES
It is common for builders and developers to offer incentives to potential purchasers. This can take various forms, such as a discount on the price, cash-back after completion or help with the deposit. Unfortunately most lenders are uncomfortable with these arrangements. In essence they suspect that the value of the property is really less than the asking price, which has been artificially inflated to allow for the incentive.

Where there is a straight discount, therefore, most lenders will simply knock the discount amount off the price and offer a mortgage based on the lower figure.

CASE STUDY

If the asking price of a property is £200,000, with a 10% discount, the lender will take the value of the property to be £180,000 and offer a mortgage on this figure – i.e. 85% of £180,000 (£153,000), not 85% of £200,000 (£170,000). In other words, the purchaser still has to find a deposit of £27,000.

In the case of a cash-back the price remains the same and a cash refund is made on or after completion. The outcome of this arrangement depends on whether the lender is aware of it. It is quite common for the offer letter (see Chapter 10) to require the purchaser's solicitor to inform the lender of any form of cash incentive. A lender informed in this way is likely to treat the arrangement as a discount by another name and deal with it as outlined above.

Help with the deposit is more likely to meet with success, with some lenders at least. Here the rule of thumb is to allow a maximum of 5% contribution from the builder. In other words, the purchaser is expected to find the remaining 10% of the 15% deposit. Only the true niche lender will accept a different formula or accept that the buyer will not provide any cash of his own at all.

If you are buying a new-build property or buying off-plan, you may well encounter this problem. A lender should be chosen with this in mind from the outset. Otherwise the problem will surface late in the transaction and could well result in the mortgage offer being withdrawn or altered in an unacceptable way.

ADVERSE CREDIT

If you have had problems securing credit in the past and are aware of such matters as defaults or county court judgments on your credit file (see Chapter 10), you need to choose a lender who does not have a problem with this and can offer a choice of adverse products. As the lender will get all the details from your file in any case, you will simply be wasting time. If you are using a broker you should make him aware of this at the outset so that he can source the appropriate lender immediately.

For a list of specialist BTL mortgage lenders, see 'Useful addresses'.

$$\boxed{7}$$

Mortgage Products

The principal products on offer in the buy-to-let (BTL) market are the following:

- discounted
- fixed
- base-rate tracker
- variable.

A discounted rate (i.e. a discount on the current variable rate) will normally be offered for a period of two or three years, after which the rate reverts to the variable. During the discount period the pay rate can move up or down in line with the lender's variable rate. It is not fixed. There will be a penalty for redeeming all or part of this mortgage during the discount period.

A fixed rate is just that – fixed, immovable. Fixed-rate terms are generally from one to five years, with the longer fixed rates the most expensive. There is a penalty for redeeming all or part of the loan during the fixed period. There may also be a non-refundable fee for booking the fixed rate at the outset.

Base-rate trackers (BRTs) are linked to the Bank of England base rate (usually 0.5–1% above) and will follow that rate up and down. They can apply for the full term of the mortgage or for a limited period. A BRT will generally be cheaper than the variable rate. Many BRTs have no redemption penalty at all. Those with a limited BRT term will usually charge a fee for redemption.

The lender's variable rate is the standard rate available on all its products. It can be varied at any time and will be more expensive than the other products offered. There are no redemption penalties.

The choice of product will depend on your circumstances but the following points are worth noting:

♦ If it is important to be able to redeem the mortgage in the early years, then the variable rate or a BRT (without a redemption penalty) are the only suitable products. The others will tie you in for a number of years with severe penalties (as high as 5%) for early redemption. This is particularly important if you think it likely that you will remortgage with another lender during the period to which the redemption penalty applies.

♦ You may be quite happy to stay with a lender for the duration of any special deal on offer. It is unlikely, however, that you will want to be tied to the same lender for a number of years after your deal has come to an end (and you are back on the lender's more expensive variable rate). That is an extended tie-in. It is surprising how often this detail is missed when a tantalisingly cheap interest rate is on offer. Extended tie-ins should be avoided at all costs. There are no free lunches!

8

Methods of Repayment

Whatever the lender and product chosen, a method of repayment needs to be selected.

There are two ways of repaying a mortgage – *capital and interest* (often called *repayment*) and *interest only*. Strictly speaking, the interest-only method doesn't repay the mortgage at all, as no capital payments are made. The outstanding balance will have to be repaid in some other way. This can be from the sale of the property, the proceeds of an investment or any other source of funds available when the mortgage is due to be redeemed. Repayment, as the term suggests, means that both capital and interest are paid throughout the term of the mortgage. At the end of the term the loan has been repaid.

REPAYMENT
The following features of this repayment method should be noted:

◆ It is the only guaranteed way of clearing the mortgage by the end of the term.

◆ Very little capital is repaid in the early years as the interest is front loaded.

◆ As capital is reduced, less interest is paid. Consequently, tax relief allowed on the mortgage interest also reduces. In the final years of the mortgage little or no interest is paid and consequently little or no tax relief is available.

INTEREST ONLY

Here, too, there are advantages and disadvantages:

- At the end of the term the entire mortgage amount is still outstanding.

- Because no capital is repaid, full tax relief is available on the mortgage interest throughout the loan term.

- The monthly outgoings are lower. Consider the following example: £100,000 borrowed over 15 years, at an interest rate of 6%, would cost £500 p.m. on an interest-only basis. On a repayment basis, however, the cost would be £843.86.

- A repayment vehicle can be put in place to clear the mortgage on completion. This can be an ISA (individual savings account), an endowment policy (now widely discredited as expensive, opaque and inefficient) or a personal pension (if you qualify for one). In all cases this will incur extra cost (something the interest-only borrower usually wants to avoid) and will involve stock market investment, with no certainty that the mortgage will be cleared.

Because of the benefits of reduced cost and tax relief, mortgage advisers frequently advise their clients to take out the loan on an interest-only basis. But this advice will not be appropriate in all cases. If, for example, the long-term objective is income in retirement this will only be possible if the mortgage is ultimately repaid. In this case a repayment mortgage is the only sensible choice.

9

The Mortgage Broker

Given the complexity of the buy-to-let (BTL) market a good mortgage broker can be of considerable benefit in sourcing the right product from the right lender. He will be up to date with the latest lending criteria, will know the lenders who have a drawdown facility or who will lend to limited companies and will know the product range in the market and where to find the maximum loan possible. The following points, however, should be noted when dealing with a mortgage broker.

TIED, PANEL OR WHOLE OF MARKET

There are three categories of mortgage broker. The *tied* broker can offer products of one lender only. This is the case for most banks and building societies. Some brokers work from a *panel* of lenders and will offer products from that panel only. Finally, there are *whole-of-market* brokers who have access to all lenders in the market. In each case the broker is obliged to declare his status at the outset.

It goes without saying given the complexities of the BTL market, that only the last category – the whole-of-market broker – should be considered by a potential BTL borrower.

REGULATED BROKERS

Since 1 November 2005 all brokers are directly regulated by the Financial Services Authority (FSA) and work under a strict set of rules and regulations.

REGULATED AND NON-REGULATED MORTGAGES

While the brokers are regulated, however, the mortgages they arrange can be regulated or non-regulated! Confused?

In their wisdom the FSA decided that not all mortgages should be regulated and only regulated mortgages should offer the borrower full protection if things go wrong. The broker and the lender must decide at the outset whether the loan is regulated or not. Among the guidelines provided to help them to decide, the following is the most important:

Will 40% of the property be occupied by the borrower or his or her immediate family? If the answer is *no* then the mortgage is *not* regulated. It is obvious, therefore, that BTL mortgages are not regulated.

The significance of this should not be underestimated. Neither the lender nor the broker is obliged to follow the strict rules of disclosure regarding such matters as fees, redemption penalties, advertising content and so forth. Nor will you be asked, for example, to state why you wish to choose an interest only mortgage or to confirm that you are aware of the associated risks. You may not receive the full, detailed key features illustration (KFI) provided for residential borrowers. You are, in effect, entering into a commercial transaction and you are deemed to be capable of looking after yourself!

ADVISED AND NON-ADVISED

Most brokers (tied, panel or whole of market) give advice on the appropriate product for your needs, based on a full analysis of the information you provide. You will encounter brokers, however, who act solely on a non-advised basis. They do not ask you to provide detailed information about your circumstances and do not offer any advice. They simply provide the product you ask for. They are obliged to inform you that you are buying a product on a non-advised or execution-only basis. It goes without saying that you have no protection whatever in these circumstances if things go wrong.

BROKERS AND PACKAGERS

A further complication when dealing with a broker is the fact that some brokers use packagers when sourcing a mortgage. A packager packages mortgages for lenders. In other words they deal with all the initial admin such as application forms, valuations, credit checks and so on, and then pass the packaged mortgage to the lender for an underwriting decision.

While some lenders see this as a useful way of attracting volume business (and reducing their costs), there are three major problems with this arrangement, from the point of view of the borrower:

◆ Interminable delays! Every lender has certain requirements in terms of paperwork, proof of income, proof of address, etc. In many cases, however, they will at least consider the case while waiting for all the paperwork to turn up. If there is a problem (unrelated to paperwork still to come) you will know about it straightaway. When a packager is used, you will not. The reason is simply that nothing is passed to the lender until absolutely every piece of paperwork is in. Only then will you know if there is a problem!

◆ Brokers who use packagers are at a serious disadvantage: they cannot talk directly to the lender. They must communicate with the packager alone and hope that they, in turn, will pass on immediately their queries to the lender. In practice they will not. The reason is simply that your case is one of hundreds the packager is dealing with. The packager has a schedule for communications with your particular lender. That may be Tuesday afternoon! In that case your broker's inquiry could well reach the lender on Tuesday afternoon, whatever the packager has told him! To describe this as inefficient would be a serious understatement.

◆ There is also the obvious handicap of never being able to talk directly to the underwriter who will make the final decision on the case. Underwriters can be persuaded to change their minds and are open to suggestions. In practice it is impossible to negotiate in this way through a packager.

BROKERS' FEES

It is not generally known that mortgage brokers are paid by the lenders in the form of a marketing allowance (or procuration fee). This will be anything from 0.25 to 1% of the mortgage amount and it is paid regardless of whether the broker charges the client a fee or not. The reason this is not generally known is because brokers do not generally tell you! And while they are now obliged to reveal this fact (in the KFI) to residential borrowers and to disclose the full cash amount received, they will not necessarily do this for the BTL borrower (see above). The point to remember is this: if you pay your broker a fee he is paid twice!

In addition to a fee payable on completion, some brokers also charge an administration fee, payable immediately and usually non-refundable. This can be anything from £100 to £500. If your broker feels the need to charge a fee before doing any work for you, how confident can he be that he will secure a mortgage?

So what should you do? The obvious answer is to find a broker who does not charge a fee. If you can't find one ask how much the broker will receive from the lender and negotiate on any fee he wishes to charge you. If the broker is reluctant to discuss these matters look for another broker.

WHERE TO FIND A BROKER

The obvious source is local and national newspaper advertising. There is, however, an organisation called IFA Promotions that carries details of independent financial advisers in your area. Their website is www.unbiased.co.uk. In this case you will know, before you start, that your broker is independent.

WHAT TO ASK

Wherever you find your mortgage broker, there are some basic questions you need to ask before you commit yourself, body and soul, to their financial advice:

- Is the broker authorised by the FSA to conduct mortgage business?
- Does he have access to the whole market?
- Does he provide advice?
- Does he charge a fee?
- What procuration fee will the broker receive from a lender?
- Does he charge an up-front admin fee?
- Does he use a packager?

If the answer to any of the first three is *no* and the answer to either of the last two is *yes*, you should definitely go elsewhere.

10

The Mortgage Process

While a full application for a mortgage can be made at the outset, there is merit in applying for a decision in principle instead. This has the advantage of time saving if the lender will not entertain the loan under any circumstances.

DECISION IN PRINCIPLE (DIP)

Most lenders offer this service. A faxed form containing the following details is all that is required at this stage:

♦ name and address
♦ income
♦ price of property
♦ mortgage required
♦ estimated rent from the property.

Armed with this information, a lender can decide if your case meets their lending criteria. They will also conduct a credit check with a credit agency to ensure that your credit history is satisfactory. A decision in 24 hours is normal.

Note, however, that if the lender agrees in principle to lend you the money, they are not in any way committed to doing so. They can change their mind for any number of reasons – from the details on the full application form to the results of the survey (see below).

WARNING!

The internet has made it possible to go directly to a lender and obtain a DIP online, in a matter of minutes. While this is very convenient, it can encourage the potential borrower to obtain decisions in principle from a number of lenders in quick succession. This can prove disastrous! For, each time a DIP is requested, the lender does a credit check (see below) and leaves a footprint on the applicant's credit file. Even if the results of the credit check are perfect, the fact that an inquiry has been made is added to the credit file and is seen by the next lender. Too many such inquiries and lenders start to turn down applications. The assumption is there must be something wrong if you are applying to so many lenders!

CREDIT CHECK

There are two credit agencies that hold details of your credit history – Equifax and Experian. Lenders will consult one or both of these for every mortgage application or DIP. Apart from basic details of name, address and date of birth, the credit file they obtain will provide the following information:

♦ Credit cards held and current balances.
♦ Payment history on credit cards for the last 12 months.
♦ Agreed limit on credit cards.
♦ Personal loans and history of payments.
♦ Mortgages held and history of payments.
♦ History of defaults on loans, mortgages or credit cards.
♦ History of late payments on loans, mortgages or credit cards.
♦ Whether a property has been repossessed or voluntarily given up.
♦ Suspected fraud at that address (e.g. fraudulent mortgage application or false identity fraud in credit card application).

- County court judgments (CCJs).
- Bankruptcies.

It is clear from the above that there is little about your financial history a lender will not know! If your history is less than perfect, it does not mean you will fail to get a mortgage. You may, however, have to try another lender.

Occasionally you will encounter a problem unexpectedly and for which the lender offers no explanation that makes sense. This can be due to incorrect information on your file. You should contact both Experian and Equifax (see 'Useful addresses') and obtain a copy of your file (the cost is nominal).

If there is incorrect information there you can arrange to have it removed. If the information is correct but you have an explanation or you think the information is misleading you can add your own comment in the appropriate place. This is called a notice of correction. The notice should not be more than 200 words and you can take advice on the wording from a solicitor, Consumer Advice Centre or Citizens' Advice Bureau. Your comments, however, should be neutral in tone. If it is a foul-mouthed attack on the lender or credit card company, it won't be published!

CREDIT SCORE

Not to be confused with a credit check, this awards marks out of ten on the basis of the lender's (usually secret) criteria. In addition to the credit check information, it will take such matters into account as age, sex, employment status, marital status, time with your bank, etc. The resulting score tells the lender whether you are the *kind* of customer they would like to have. Only a few lenders still bother with a credit score.

ILLUSTRATION

If you are dealing with a broker you should be given an illustration before you complete a mortgage application form. If you are applying directly to the lender you should receive an illustration by return post. As a buy-to-let (BTL) mortgage is not a regulated product, however (see Chapter 9), you may not receive a full key features illustration (KFI). This largely depends on the lender from whom the illustration is obtained. Whichever version you receive you should note carefully the following details:

♦ Arrangement *fees*, valuation fees, any booking fees, higher lending fees and fees paid by the lender to the broker are set out clearly in cash terms. Also included will be any fee you have agreed to pay the broker yourself. If you receive an old-style illustration (as opposed to a full KFI), the lender's fee to the broker will be referred to but not detailed and any fee you pay to the broker will not even be referred to.

♦ Naturally you will expect to find the *interest rate* in the illustration but you will also find the term of any lower initial rate and the rate it will revert to when the term ends.

♦ The initial *monthly cost* will be stated plus the monthly cost after any initial lower-rate ends.

♦ With any special deal (such as an initial discounted rate) the *penalty for redeeming* the mortgage (or part thereof) during this time will be set out in cash terms (the full KFI) or as a percentage of the amount redeemed (old-style illustration).

◆ You will be reminded of which *repayment method* – capital and interest or interest only – you have chosen.

◆ Also provided is a *table of monthly costs* for each month over the entire mortgage plus the total cost (i.e. the capital plus interest paid).

THE APPLICATION

At this point a full application form will be completed. This is considerably more searching than the DIP form and asks for more detailed information. In the case of addresses, for example, most lenders look for a three-year history and will want all addresses relevant for that period. If there is a gap they can't account for, they may assume you have been in prison and turn you down!

In the case of self-employed applicants, a few lenders may ask, at this point, for details of an accountant or book-keeper. In the absence of one they may require proof that tax returns have been submitted. This is rare for BTL lenders but it can arise. If it is likely to be a problem, a good broker will steer you well clear of such lenders.

ONLINE APPLICATION

It is increasingly common for applications to be made online, whether the application is made direct to the lender or through a broker. This has the obvious advantage of speed but does not entirely remove the need for paperwork. Some lenders may require certified copies of money-laundering requirements (see below) or original signatures on a direct debit form. If so, these will have to follow by post.

MONEY LAUNDERING

It is a mystery how anyone could launder money by borrowing it! Lenders, however, must act as if it is a daily occurrence. Accordingly, you will need to produce proof of ID (a passport) and proof of address (recent utility bill, bank statement, mortgage statement or council tax bill). Original documents in all cases.

VALUATION/SURVEY

The valuation fee, payable to the lender (by cheque or credit card), will be sent in with the application form. This fee will be refunded if, for any reason, the valuation does not take place. However, once the valuer has done his job there can be no refund of his fee, even if the mortgage is subsequently declined.

As for the valuation itself, the borrower has a choice. He can opt for a simple valuation, a homebuyer's report or a full structural survey.

Valuation

The valuation, the cheapest option (and chosen by most BTL borrowers) is just that – a valuation. The purpose of the report is to check that the property is worth the price to be paid for it. Only obvious defects, such as subsidence, structural problems or essential repairs, will be noted.

Homebuyer's report

The homebuyer's report is more expensive and this is as much for the benefit of the borrower as the lender. The report will be considerably more detailed than a simple valuation and will highlight such matters as poor window frames, peeling paintwork, etc.

Full structural

The full structural is the most thorough and most expensive of all. This will cover everything from the state of the roof timbers to the condition of the floor under the carpets.

THE UNDERWRITING PROCESS

Once the underwriter has received all the paperwork, he will assess the case in detail. If a decision in principle has already been made, the underwriter will compare the information on the DIP form with that on the more detailed application form. Any discrepancy here could give rise to concern and a request for clarification. If the underwriter is unhappy, he could decline the application and halt the process here. If all is well, he will instruct a valuer. When the valuation report is back, the underwriter will assess its contents. If he is happy with that, he will proceed to the offer stage.

VALUER'S REPORT

This is crucial. In the case of a BTL mortgage, the valuer has to provide the lender with two pieces of information – the *value* he puts on the property and his assessment of *the rent* it would fetch.

From the borrower's point of view, *both* figures have to be right! As far as the price is concerned, this naturally has to correspond to the value of the property as set by the valuer. In a stable or rising market this is normally not a problem. The valuer will set a value at the price offered, though never higher! In a volatile or falling market, however, the valuer may come in at a fractionally lower level (e.g. 5% lower) in order to cover himself against future falls in the market. In this case the wisest course of action is to provide the vendor with the valuer's figures and renegotiate the price. A sensible vendor will reduce the price to the valuer's figure. After all, if the vendor starts again with a new purchaser, he is likely to face the same problem (and quite possibly the same valuer!).

In the case of the rent assessment, the situation is altogether different. Most valuers have no idea how to assess the rental figure for any given property. Because the BTL market is relatively young, many valuers have little or no experience of setting rental values. In some cases they will check with local letting agents and settle on a figure slightly lower than the average (to be on the safe side!). Others will ask the selling agent what they think it will fetch. If the property is already let, the valuer will want to know the rent. In all cases two points are worth noting:

◆ Always tell the valuer (directly or through the selling agent) *what rent you believe can be achieved.* Never forget to do this. In many cases he will accept your figures.

◆ If the rental figure in the report is lower than you need, always *appeal.* Even a slight reduction in the monthly rental figure needed for the mortgage could make the purchase impossible. An appeal is always worth making.

To appeal a rental valuation, you will need to contact at least two local letting agents and ask for a rental assessment on their company letterheads (there will normally be little trouble obtaining these as local agents will hope to do business with you in the future). In addition to the rental assessments, however, the agents will need to state in writing that they currently receive a similar rent for a similar property in the same area. A valuer might well ask for such details. Without them, the valuer may ignore the agents' assessments altogether. Armed with appropriate and detailed evidence, however, most valuers will change their minds and adjust their figures.

THE OFFER

This is what everyone is waiting for. The lender sends out a formal offer letter to the borrower, with a copy to his solicitor.

A cursory glance at any offer letter reveals the one-sided nature of the document. Apart from the basic details of the loan amount, interest rate, repayment term, redemption penalties, etc., it is all about the lender's rights and the borrower's responsibilities! A typical offer will cover the following:

- The right of the lender to withdraw the offer at any time before completion.

- The lender's right to repossess if certain conditions are not met.

- The responsibility of the borrower to insure the building, keep it in a reasonable state, pay all local taxes, pay any ground rent or service charges.

In addition, the special nature of a BTL mortgage will require the inclusion of further conditions and duties specific to the *rental aspect* of the transaction. The following could reasonably be expected in a BTL offer letter:

- The requirement that the property be let within a specified term of the loan release – typically, three months.

- The requirement that the property be let (i.e. not used by yourself) for the duration of the mortgage.

- If the property is already let, the tenancy agreement must be acceptable to the lender.

- Acceptable tenancies are assured shorthold tenancies of 6 or 12 months. No other kind can be used (unless the lender allows borrowers to let to local authorities or housing associations; see below).

- The exclusion of specific tenant groups such as students, housing associations or local authorities.

- Where these groups are not excluded, special conditions may be imposed. For example, when letting to local authorities or housing associations a maximum term of three years is commonly set. Because anything can happen in a three-year period, the lender will try to build in further protection for themselves. The offer letter may require, for example, that the borrower give irrevocable authority to the housing association or local authority to pay the rent directly to the lender if the lender asks him to do so. This covers the lender against the possibility that the borrower fails to make his mortgage payments but the lender can't repossess until the three-year term is up. Lenders can take the rent in the meantime and repossess later. Lenders don't miss a trick!

BUILDINGS INSURANCE

Before a lender will release mortgage funds, a suitable buildings insurance policy will have to be in place. The solicitor for the purchaser will need to provide the lender with details of the policy. Failure to do this can hold up the entire process.

Not only must a policy be in place, but it must also be the *right* policy. For a BTL lender only a BTL policy will do – a policy that specifically recognises that the property will be let and not owner occupied. An ordinary policy would provide no cover at all as the insurance company would simply refuse to meet a claim.

TRANSFER OF FUNDS

Once the borrower's solicitor has satisfied the lender as to title and confirmed that buildings insurance is in place, funds can be transferred and the mortgage is complete.

11

Bridging Finance

Bridging finance is a stop-gap measure to solve a problem – how to complete on the purchase of a property when the sale of your own has not yet been finalised or when a mortgage on the new property has yet to materialise. It is a temporary measure (never open-ended) and has been traditionally provided by the banks.

For the property investor, the need for bridging finance is most likely to arise following a successful bid at an auction (auction catalogues routinely carry advertisements for bridging loan companies). When a property is bought at auction, 10% of the price is paid immediately in cash and the balance is due 28 days later. If a mortgage hasn't already been arranged (and it rarely can be), it must be put in place before the deadline for completion. Failure to meet this deadline will result in the loss of the deposit. It then gets worse. If the property is subsequently sold for less than your bid, you could be liable for the shortfall!

Most lenders simply don't work fast enough for this. A valuation needs to be arranged, the searches made, the offer issued, the legal work completed and the funds transferred. In the meantime, anything can go wrong. A poor valuation report can play havoc with the timetable. The lender may retain some funds until essential work is carried out. The valuer may call for an engineer's report, resulting in further delays and expense. Some lenders can take five working days just to transfer funds! For this

reason many successful bidders at auction find themselves turning
to the providers of bridging finance.

MISCONCEPTIONS

Let us first deal with the widespread misconceptions about
bridging finance:

- It is not a mortgage. *Wrong*. It is a mortgage.
- It is very fast and simple. *Wrong*. It is a mortgage.
- It is expensive. *Wrong*. It is a horrendously expensive mortgage.

No lender will happily advance many thousands of pounds without
security. A loan secured on a property is a mortgage. Bridging
finance is a mortgage. Even if the loan will be needed for a very
short time, the lender will still require a charge on a property so that
they can recover their loan if the borrower defaults.

By definition, therefore, it is not a simple process and, while it is
faster than a traditional mortgage, it is not at all as fast as is
commonly believed. All the normal requirements of a mortgage
are there:

- Proof of ID and address.
- Satisfactory valuation.
- Proof of title.
- Buildings insurance.
- Registration of mortgage deeds.

Having said that, specialist bridging finance companies do tend to
work faster than the banks by, for example, insuring the title to

the property instead of conducting searches through the local authorities. Such searches can add weeks to the mortgage process. Again, specialist firms will tend to arrange valuations very quickly and move the whole process along at a brisker pace than the banks. While a bank can take up to three or four weeks to arrange the loan, a bridging finance company could achieve the same result in, perhaps, seven working days if all the requirements listed above can be met in that time (claims for a shorter timescale than this should not be believed). They have, after all, a powerful incentive to move quickly – their fees.

BRIDGING FINANCE COSTS

The costs that can be incurred in obtaining bridging finance are staggering. Consider the following.

Interest rates

Rates are set on a monthly basis and can range from 1.25% to 1.5% per month. These are credit card rates! A typical mortgage would cost a third of this.

Fees

In addition to the standard valuation fee and your own legal costs you can expect the following:

◆ *Solicitor's fees*: not *your* solicitor's, the lender's! It is standard practice to require the borrower to pay all the lender's expenses, including their solicitor's costs. Unfortunately these costs are not the standard conveyancing costs prevalent in the mortgage industry. While solicitors charge a flat fee for their work in relation to a routine mortgage, they base their bridging finance fees on the value of the property! You can expect to pay two or three times the normal rate.

◆ *Broker's fee*: if you are using a broker to arrange the bridging loan, he will be paid by the lender but *you* will pay the fee to the lender. This is usually 1% of the loan. It is not possible to avoid this as no bridging finance provider will pay the broker's costs.

◆ *Redemption fee*: this is paid when the loan is redeemed and is typically one or two months' interest. In other words, you can expect a redemption fee of between 1.25 and 3% of the loan.

CASE STUDY

Consider the example of a £350,000 bridging loan taken out for just one month:

One month's interest at 1.25%	4,375
Lender's legal fees	1,200
Broker's fee	3,500
Redemption fee (2 months' interest)	8,750
Total	**£17,825**

These figures could change dramatically if the interest rate charged is higher or the loan is out for more than a month. It is quite common for lenders to insist on a minimum loan period of, say, three months. In the above example, this would bring the total cost to an eye-watering £26,575! This could more than wipe out any possible savings made by buying at auction.

Penalty fee

If the loan is not redeemed in full at the end of the maximum term agreed the lender can add a penalty fee to the outstanding balance (typically 5% of the amount borrowed) and levy the charge again on each anniversary of the start date of the loan.

LENDING CRITERIA

As with mortgages there are standard criteria that apply to virtually all bridging loans.

Maximum loan

Given these indecent profit margins, you might expect lenders to be generous with their loan-to-value criteria. Not so. The maximum loan you can expect is 70%. This is belt and braces for the lender. If you fail to redeem the loan the property will be sold with the absolute certainty that the lender will recover the debt, and all related expenses, in full.

The term

A typical term is 12 months, with the loan to be repaid in full at the end. Normally there will be the right to redeem the loan earlier, but watch out for the *minimum term* requirement. Many bridging loan companies insist that you keep the loan for a certain period, typically three months (see above). This insures a guaranteed overall profit on each transaction. You can't redeem the loan even if you are able to do so!

Non-status

Unlike mortgages, most bridging loans are not based on your ability to repay the loan. They are, in the jargon, 'non-status loans'. Income, therefore, is not a factor in deciding whether you should get a bridging loan or not. At the same time, confusingly, application forms for such loans do ask about employment details and income. It is important at the outset to establish that your loan will indeed be non-status unless, of course, you have sufficient income to service the loan, together with you current mortgage and all other liabilities!

WHERE TO FIND A BRIDGING LOAN

There are two sources for such loans – banks and bridging loan companies.

Banks

As a general rule you should approach your bank in the first instance and go elsewhere only if you are turned down. The possible benefits are as follows:

♦ A lower interest rate. The rate will still be very high but in most cases lower (though not by much!) than the prevailing rates elsewhere.

♦ Lower fees. As a general rule, banks will charge a single arrangement fee, typically 1%, and are unlikely to hit you with punitive legal costs.

Unfortunately, that's where the good news ends. Banks can pose problems:

♦ They can be slow. If speed is of the essence you may fall at the first hurdle.

♦ Banks don't like an open bridge. This is where there is no clear and definite date for redeeming the loan. In practice this means your bank may want to see a mortgage offer from another lender before they will agree to do the bridge. But if you have a mortgage offer, you are almost there!

Bridging loan companies

Here you have to tread carefully. Bridging loan companies come in various guises and it is very important to distinguish between them at the outset.

The most common error is to mistake a broker for a lender. This is very easy to do as many intermediaries use trade names which clearly suggest that they are principals rather than agents. You could be some way down the application process before realising your mistake. Does this matter? Yes, for two reasons:

- You will incur a broker fee of at least 1%.

- You are not dealing directly with the lender, thus running the serious risk of delays and misunderstandings.

If you are answering an advertisement ask, at the outset, if you are talking to a *principal* lender. If you are looking at a website, don't neglect to press the 'About us' or the 'Corporate profile' button for this vital information.

If you have no luck with your bank, a simple Google search on the internet is undoubtedly the quickest way to draw up a short list of bridging loan companies. Other sources are advertisements in auction catalogues and the financial pages of national newspapers.

THE SCAMS

Bridging finance applicants are always in a hurry and sometimes desperate. They can be exploited.

You might imagine that extortionate fees and crippling interest rates would be reward enough for those in the bridging finance sector. Think again!

Unrealistic timescale

The most common device to lure the unwary is to promise a completion date of just a few days. For the reasons we have already seen this is rarely, if ever, possible. Having embarked on an application, however, you are not going to start again elsewhere. Time has already been lost. You will continue with the application.

The last-minute demand

This is perhaps the most brutal and cynical exercise of power over the weak and vulnerable. But it does happen and you need to guard against it. It works like this.

Your application proceeds without a problem and you are close to completion. Suddenly you get a call from someone you had never heard of. He has been asked to look over your application before funds are released. He has a problem. He has noticed something in the valuation report which seems unusual, or his solicitor tells him there is some question mark over title. He will have to check with his insurer. If they are not happy they may recommend an additional fee to reflect the additional risk. Could you ring back in 20 minutes?

In reality there is no problem and no insurer to satisfy. If there were a real problem of any sort, the application would not be accepted at all. Simply charging a fee to cover a real risk would make no commercial sense whatever, and bridging finance companies take no risks at all with their security.

The reason you are asked to call back later is twofold: you need time to get used to and accept the idea that you will have to pay even more for the loan and, secondly, you will show your desperation by ringing *them*! You are now ready for the slaughter and offering your neck to the knife. What choice do you have? You are certainly not going elsewhere at this stage.

THE PROCESS

Since a bridging loan is, in effect, a mortgage, formalities are inescapable. Because such loans are non-status, however, and speed is of the essence, paperwork tends to be minimal and the lender moves swiftly to secure a charge on the property.

Paperwork

The application form should require little more than name, address, details of current mortgage lender and solicitor, together with a signed authorisation to conduct credit reference checks. If anyone else aged 18 or over also lives in the property, the lender will want him to sign a mortgage consent form, effectively agreeing to the mortgage and waiving any right to remain in the property should the lender require possession. Details of current buildings insurance will be required, and you will need to ask the insurer to note the new lender's interest. Failure to get this piece of paperwork at an early stage can hold up the entire process.

Lenders who ask for more paperwork than the above should be treated with extreme caution. You may encounter the following:

- ◆ A requirement that the borrower write a letter (in his own handwriting) stating that he does not wish to use his own bank for a bridging loan.

- A further statement, again in the borrower's own handwriting, stating that he can afford the loan repayments from his income.

As the loan is non-status, affordability is not an issue and the loan will not be repaid from income. As for the reference to banks, you might well wonder what experience other borrowers have had with such a lender and whether you should proceed any further.

Valuation

As in the case of a mortgage, a valuation will be required. If the amount to be borrowed is well below any likely valuation, the lender may settle for a drive-by valuation which does not require a visit and costs a good deal less than a normal valuation.

Independent legal advice

A reputable lender will advise in writing, at the outset, that independent legal advice should be sought before proceeding. Have nothing to do with a lender who does not follow this practice.

Mortgage deed

The last stage before completion is the signing of the mortgage deed. This will usually be witnessed by your solicitor.

Release of funds

Normally through the lender's solicitor direct to your solicitor's bank account.

TIP

Given the cost and the risks involved, every effort should be made to avoid bridging loans altogether. Try your bank first. It won't gouge your eyes out! If you have to use a specialist lender, look out for scams and extortionate fees. Ask if you are dealing with an agent or principal lender. Ask if the lender has ever subsequently asked for fees additional to those quoted in the initial offer letter. If you are using a broker, check that he has used this lender before and ask for details. If he hasn't used this lender, find another broker. If he hasn't arranged a bridging loan before, find another broker. Watch out for strange requests such as handwritten letters indemnifying the lender. Go elsewhere. Don't accept the interest rate and charges quoted. Negotiate better terms.

Part Three

Properties

12

Your Objective

So what sort of property to buy and where? At this point you have to decide what you want to achieve – capital growth, yield (or both) and over what term.

CAPITAL GROWTH

Straightforward enough. If you buy for £100,000 and sell for £200,000 you have capital growth of £100,000 and can feel very pleased with yourself. However, there is no certainty of capital growth (a sudden downturn in the market can put paid to that) and, in some cases, you would be wise to expect none at all from the outset.

This is particularly so for certain types of properties in certain areas. For example, whole streets of little terraced houses in rundown parts of the north and the Midlands are frequently bought for next to nothing by local estate agents or developers and sold on for a quick profit, with DSS tenants already in place (social housing tenants only because other tenants don't want such properties). The attraction for the purchaser is the high rental yield (see below), but any claims of future growth should be treated with derision. Nobody wants these properties. Only another investor (possibly believing the tall tales of capital growth) would consider buying them.

Conversely, there are areas where growth, given the right conditions, could be expected to be greater than average and achieved sooner than elsewhere. Central London is the obvious example. It is a truism to say that, when the market moves it moves first in central London. The downside, of course, is the pitiful rental yield. There are no free lunches.

Apart from central London (where you just have to sit patiently and wait for the action), what can you do to improve your chances of capital growth? The one-word answer is research.

Town hall planning department

First, check the planning department of the local town hall. Has the mental hospital been sold to a property developer (care in the community!) and are there plans for a housing development? Perhaps what used to be a local council department of education has been sold and is set for redevelopment. Other clear indicators of future growth are plans for new transport links, by rail or road, new shopping centres, new supermarkets. Information on these and any other developments are freely available at the planning department of the local town hall. This should be your first port of call.

Land Registry

Information on prices (by region, county, borough and local authority) is available directly from the Land Registry on www.landreg.gov.uk.

The web

The Land Registry has spawned a variety of websites offering information and analysis of all sorts, mostly based on Land Registry data. Check the following:

www.houseprices.co.uk
www.myhouseprice.com
www.upmystreet.com
www.hometrack.co.uk
www.nationwide.co.uk/hpi
www.housepricecrash.co.uk
www.ourproperty.co.uk
uk.realestate.yahoo.com

The Association of Residential Letting Agents (ARLA)

The ARLA (see 'Useful addresses') produces regular reports on the state of the buy-to-let market throughout the country.

YIELD

This is essentially the rent received as a percentage of the price paid for the property. If a property, bought for £100,000, commands a rent of £10,000 p.a., then the yield is 10%. This is, however, the *gross* yield. To arrive at the *net* figure, running costs (such as interest payments on the mortgage, repairs and agents' fees) should be deducted from the rent. It is clear that the net figure is the one that really matters. If, in the case of the £100,000 purchase above, the annual costs are £6,500 then the net yield is just 3.5%. If the rent, however, were only £5,000 p.a. then the yield has effectively disappeared. In this case you are not covering your costs and will have to find the difference from your own resources. When you consider further that there will be an income tax liability to deal with, then a potential gross yield of anything less than 6% should be treated with great caution.

INVESTMENT TERM

Property investment should always be for the long term, with 10 years the recommended minimum. Clearly, the longer the term the greater the chances of achieving capital growth. It follows that, if a shorter term is envisaged, great care is needed in the choice of property. It may be that a much lower yield than usual will be acceptable in the hope of greater capital growth over the shorter term. As a general rule there is a straight trade-off between the two. The higher the yield, the lower the likely growth and vice versa. Alternatively, a property that could be quickly and cheaply improved might produce an instant gain in the right market conditions.

Student Houses

As a general rule, flats (or 'apartments' as estate agents are increasingly calling them) provide a better yield than houses. They are cheaper to buy and rents are relatively high. A three-bedroom house might fetch about the same rent as the much cheaper two or three-bedroom flat. The one exception to this rule is when the house is let to sharers, as opposed to a family. The most common example of this is student accommodation – the student house. Because students (i.e. their parents) pay per room, the overall rent for a student house is considerably greater than would normally be the case. Hence the exceptionally high yield.

Every September, in university towns and cities throughout the country, hordes of eager young students move in to their accommodation for the next academic year. While many first-year students will be moving into university halls of residence, most second and third years will be moving into privately rented houses. Without the private rented sector universities would be in dire straits. With tertiary education continuing to expand year on year, the opportunities for the private landlord are considerable.

So, how do you tap into this lucrative market?

HOW TO BUY
First, choose a university town. Next, locate the university on the map. Now check both prices and rents in the surrounding area, taking care to calculate the rent on a room-by-room basis. At this

stage a simple search on the sales and rentals section of a website like www.fish4homes.co.uk will give you all the information you need. If average prices are not too high and rents (per room, remember) not too low, then you might decide the potential yield is sufficient for your purpose. If it doesn't work, move to another town.

Next, contact the accommodation department of the university itself. You will find them very helpful. Tell them you are planning to buy and ask for advice. You need to know the following:

◆ Is there currently enough private accommodation for students, and does the university itself have plans for expanding its own provision?

◆ What is the average rent per student, per room?

◆ What streets or areas do students prefer and what areas should be avoided?

◆ What time of the year do students start looking for accommodation and when are house lists handed out to them?

◆ Does the accommodation department have its own website for students?

◆ What does the university require of landlords before adding their property to the house lists and websites (e.g. sight of gas safety certificates, etc.)?

If your research and calculations point to a viable student letting scenario there are still a few more considerations to make before looking for a suitable property.

WHEN TO BUY

Most students start looking for property in March for the autumn term and most will have sorted themselves out by May or June. There is no point, therefore, in completing your purchase in, say, July or August. Although you are on time for the September intake of students, most of these will have their accommodation arranged already. You will be relying on stragglers to fill your rooms. Ideally, therefore, complete your purchase by March.

WHAT TO BUY

Buy cheap terraced houses as close as possible to the university. The important criteria are cost, number of rooms and location. Always take the university's advice on location and don't choose a house because you would like to live there yourself! If you do, it is almost certainly the wrong choice.

OVER THE PASSAGE

In some towns and cities cheap terraced houses have a further advantage. Although nominally, for example, three bedroom, their layout can convert them to four. These properties are over-the-passage terraced houses. A passage by the side of the house allows access to the back of the house without going through the front door. The front door, in such houses, leads directly to the front room. This becomes a perfectly usable additional bedroom. A four-bedroom house for the price of a three!

Sometimes one passage serves four or five houses, allowing access to all their back doors. While the house *you* are interested in, therefore, may not itself have a side passage, it may benefit from a passage further along the terrace. Such information will not appear on a typical website or typical agent's handout. You will have to ask.

HMOs

Letting to students will frequently mean having to comply with the rules and regulations governing HMOs (or Houses of Multiple Occupation). Great care needs to be taken in this regard (see Chapter 22).

Flats and Leases

LEASEHOLD AND FREEHOLD

There is an important legal distinction in the way flats and houses
are owned in the UK. Flats (whether conversions or purpose
built) are invariably leasehold, while houses are freehold. The flat
owner, in effect, buys a lease on the property. In return he or she
pays a ground rent to the landlord who retains the freehold of the
building. The distinction is important because the leaseholder is
bound by the terms and conditions of the lease. Great care needs
to be taken to avoid being unnecessarily restricted by unexpected
conditions. It is your solicitor's task to examine the lease. In
practice, however, most solicitors are unaware of the particular
requirements of investors (as opposed to residential purchasers)
and can easily miss quite crucial details. Look out in particular
for the following.

Permission to sublet

The lease may require permission from the freeholder before the
property can be let. He can refuse permission. Your solicitor
should request this permission in writing before exchanging
contracts. It is worth noting that when you, in turn, come to sell,
your purchaser will be faced with the same problem.

Unusual letting restrictions

New leases should be checked with great care. A developer may
have some strange ideas about their new block and its future
occupants. He may, for example, try to control the tone of the

building by restricting sublets to couples only (thus avoiding the more volatile sharer market). If you buy a three-bedroom flat with a lease like that, you are in trouble. Even a one or two-bedroom flat in these circumstances should be avoided. Breach of the terms of the lease is a hanging offence. You could lose the property.

LEASE TERM

Typical lease terms are 99 years at the outset. Unless the flat is a new build, therefore, the term will have shrunk by the time you come to buy it. Does it matter how many years are left on the lease at the time of purchase? Yes, for three reasons:

- Lenders require that there should be at least 25 years left after the mortgage has been repaid. In the case of a 25-year mortgage, therefore, only a 50-year plus term will be acceptable.

- In the marketplace, residential purchasers do not like leases of less than 80 years and will generally avoid them. If you buy a flat with a lease of, say, 82 years and plan to sell after five, you will be faced with this problem. Residential purchasers may be your primary market at that time.

- A lease can be extended with permission of the freeholder who cannot legally withhold this permission. He will, however, charge for the privilege and the cost could be significant. The shorter the remaining term, the higher the cost. Disputes are common in this area and the matter is frequently resolved by a tribunal. In essence the freeholder sees lease extensions, along with any service charges (see Chapter 16), as a useful source of additional revenue. The question for you is whether you want to help him get rich at your expense. In the case of the 82-year lease above, you will almost certainly need to extend this before you sell.

COMMONHOLD

Only recently created by the Commonhold and Leasehold Reform Act 2002 and implemented in 2004, this form of flat ownership sweeps aside the traditional leasehold system altogether and gives the owner absolute title to the flat. There is no landlord and no lease. The owner becomes a 'unit-holder' in the block and a member of the 'commonhold association' which manages the building. It is a vast improvement on the leasehold system and removes all the disadvantages associated with it. It is, however, extremely rare and will take many years to become established.

THE FREEHOLD FLAT

Not to be confused with share of freehold (see Chapter 15) or 'commonhold' (see above), this is a rare creature in the property world but it can be encountered from time to time. In this case there is no lease at all and the flat itself is freehold. While this might sound ideal it is, in fact, a complete headache for the purchaser. The problem is that there is no *common* freeholder for all the flats in the block and therefore no one responsible for maintaining the building itself. Unlike the new commonhold system there is no 'commonhold association' and there are no 'unit-holders'. As a result, lenders will not lend on such properties.

15

Conversions

PROS AND CONS

As the term suggests, conversions are created from what was once a family house. Typically there will be just two or three flats in the building. There are several clear advantages for the investor in opting for a conversion:

- Tenants prefer them.
- They are usually more spacious.
- There are no service charges (see Chapter 16).
- It is quite common to find they are for sale with a share-of-freehold (see below).

Against this should be set two potential disadvantages:

- The conversion itself. Some early conversions may not have been carried out to a high standard. A problem of this nature, however, will usually be picked up by the survey.

- The common parts of the building (stairs and hallway) are the responsibility of all the owners (neither your tenants nor the freeholder of the building will want to know!). So who keeps these areas clean? The answer, in many cases, is nobody. You may have to pop round from time to time with your dustpan and brush!

CONVERSIONS AND SHARE-OF-FREEHOLD

A neat solution to any problems posed by the lease (see Chapter 14) is to purchase a share of the freehold, if it is available, at the same time as you buy the leasehold. In practice this opportunity only arises in the case of a conversion where the freehold was split, at the time of conversion, among the occupants of the building (usually a former family house). Where the opportunity arises it is wise to take it. The principal reasons are as follows:

◆ No ground rent. While the lease will stipulate a ground rent, there is little point in paying it to yourself!

◆ The term of the lease is now academic. As a freeholder you can extend the lease, in agreement with the other freeholders, whenever you choose and at nominal cost.

There is just one disadvantage in having a share of the freehold: you really must get on well with the other freeholders! The reason is that you will all *have to agree* before anything can be done. If the roof needs replacing and there is an independent freeholder, it is his job to get the estimates, arrange the work and charge each leaseholder his share. When you share the freehold you must do this together. The best solution is for the freeholders to set up a sinking fund so that there is always cash available for essential repairs and maintenance to the common areas. In addition, after taking legal advice, a separate freehold company could be set up. There is a price for freedom but, in most cases, it is well worth paying.

16

Purpose Built

SERVICE CHARGE

From the investor's point of view, the essential drawback with a
purpose-built flat is the service charge. Unlike the ground rent
which is payable on all leasehold properties and is both modest
and fixed, the service charge is anything but. In principle the
charge is there to take care of the building's maintenance costs
and is set annually.

There are two problems with this charge:

♦ As it is an extra cost to the investor, it can play havoc with the
  potential yield, sometimes making the investment too risky.

♦ There is the added factor of future uncertainty. The freeholder
  or his managing agent can set any level they like and raise it
  annually by whatever sum they choose. It is difficult, if not
  downright impossible, to challenge the level of the charge.
  Most leaseholders find that the price they pay bears little
  relation to any maintenance work carried out on the building.
  In short, the service charge has become a nice little earner for
  many freeholders. This is the main reason why legislation has
  been introduced to enable some leaseholders to buy out the
  freehold of their building. It was also a factor in the creation
  of the new commonhold system of tenure (see Chapter 14).

It has to be said, however, that conversions are not always easy to
find, and a flat in a block may be your only choice. So what

precautions can you take? There is only one practical thing you can do: ask to see the record of service charges for the last five years. This will give you some idea of what you might expect over the next five. If these are not provided, don't buy the flat. If it is a newly built flat you will have to decide what level of risk you wish to take (see Chapter 18).

THE BLOCK

Purpose-built flats, by definition, form part of a block. While most private blocks present no problem for lenders or residential purchasers, they can hold a hidden danger for the investor: if the block is very large or forms part of a large development, you will be competing for tenants with many other landlords. This will drive rents down or, worse still, leave you without a tenant. Local agents will struggle to fill the flats. This problem can be further exacerbated if the developer of the block actively markets his flats to the BTL investor (see Chapter 18).

EX-LOCAL AUTHORITY

Most towns and cities in the UK have their share of local authority apartment blocks. Over the years many of these flats have been sold at a substantial discount to their tenants. In many cases they, in turn, have sold on at a substantial profit. This process continues today and there is an active market in ex-local authority flats.

There are several advantages for the BTL investor:

◆ These flats are substantially cheaper than comparable flats in the private sector, while rents are the same or higher. There is thus a better yield from the outset.

◆ Many blocks are located in central areas, close to transport and shopping centres and, for this reason, are favoured by tenants.

◆ They are usually more spacious than their private counterparts – another reason for their appeal to the tenant market.

So, is there a downside? Unfortunately, yes. The problem lies with mortgage lenders. While most lenders have no problem with ex-local *houses*, many still shy away from flats. The reason is the perception, still prevalent in the mortgage market, that ex-local authority flats are difficult to sell. If the lender has to foreclose, therefore, he may have trouble recovering his mortgage. If there is a problem in this respect, however, it is precisely because lenders are reluctant to lend on these properties in the first place! Be that as it may, there is a problem here to be overcome. The solution for the investor is to choose only those flats that lenders will consider and ignore the rest. So, what do lenders object to?

Height of the building

You may well wonder why lenders should care! The fact is, however, that *five storeys* is the limit for most lenders. Blocks of 10 to 20 storeys are a definite no no. Note also that it makes no difference if your flat is on the ground floor. It is the number of storeys in the building that counts. The exception to this five-storey rule is when the price of the flat is above a certain figure set by the lender – for example, £300,000 (presumably because properties of this value will be highly desirable for one reason or another).

Mix of occupants

Many lenders will only accept a mortgage application if the number of owner occupants in the block is already at least 50%.

How do they know what the figure is? The short answer is they have no idea! They will rely entirely on the valuer for this information. How does the valuer know? The short answer is he has no idea either and will not take the trouble to find out! However, there is a real danger that the valuer will make a guesstimate when he does his valuation and include that figure in the report. If that figure is less than 50% you will not get your mortgage. So what do you do?

Contact the housing department of the local council and ask them for occupancy figures. Pass on these figures immediately to the selling agent (who will normally be completely ignorant of such matters and their significance) and ask for contact details for the valuer so that you can pass on these figures directly. The valuer will invariably accept your figures without question. So much for the science of valuation!

Concrete overcoat
If the surface of the block is clad with concrete slabs, forget about a mortgage. Lenders are suspicious about this type of construction (quite common in the 1950s and 1960s) and won't lend on flats in such buildings. If there is any concrete at all on the surface of the building you are interested in, contact the local council and ask for the technical data on the construction. Pass this information on to the lender before embarking on a valuation and check if they have any objections.

Balcony access
Some buildings have external walkways that provide access to the front doors of the flats. Many lenders dislike this. They will lend only if the flats are accessed from inside the building. Again, check with the lender before paying for a valuation.

Auction Properties

It is the prospect of a bargain that draws buyers to auctions (whether property auctions or any other kind), and auction houses are only too keen to promote this aspect of their business. For the property investor the attraction is obvious. If a property can be bought for less than its true value on the open market, then the investor is already on his way to a painless capital gain.

Then there is issue of speed. For both vendor and purchaser, the process is complete in seconds! Compare that with the endless business of selling on the open market with the risk of gazumping, gazundering or a simple change of mind, any time before exchange of contracts.

It is the aspect of speed, more than anything else, which draws certain vendors to the auction houses. Most important, from the bidder's point of view are executor sales and repossession sales. These are important because they offer a perfectly simple and transparent reason for appearing at auction in the first place – speed. The executors of an estate do not have time to indulge in the lengthy and quaint process of English property conveyancing. Likewise, banks and building societies want their mortgage repaid immediately. They don't care if the price paid is less than it might otherwise be, so long as the outstanding mortgage is cleared and any shortfall covered by indemnity insurance. It is these two areas that offer the best prospects of a bargain for the property auction bidder.

But what are the wrong reasons for a property's appearance in an auction catalogue? There are basically two, both posing potential risks for the successful bidder – the property and the tenants.

THE PROPERTY

Many properties are best sold at auction because they are difficult or impossible to sell otherwise. Lenders may be willing to provide a mortgage on these properties but they are in such poor decorative condition overall that buyers are put off as soon as they see them. A vendor, unwilling to spend the necessary money on such a property, will take it to auction.

There is, however, another category of auction property that poses a serious risk for the unwary bidder. These properties have one thing in common – lenders will not readily provide a mortgage for them. Here are the reasons.

Structural problems

Many properties at auction have serious problems. Some of these problems are such that a lender will not readily advance funds to purchase them. Few lenders decline a mortgage altogether because of the property, but when they do the problems are severe and usually structural. There may, for example, be evidence of subsidence. As most people need a mortgage to buy, this makes the property effectively unsaleable.

Planning problems

Work may have been carried out in the property without the appropriate planning or building regulation permission (perhaps a loft conversion or new extension). Sometimes a lender will regard this so seriously that they will require the matter be resolved with the planning department before they will consider a mortgage. Again, no mortgage, no sale.

DIY conversions

In a category of its own is the makeshift conversion of a building into separate apartments. Not only has planning permission not been obtained but there are also obvious issues of safety and, of course, the matter of local council tax infringements. A lender won't lend on the property in that condition. It will have to be restored to its original condition or, in the absence of a willing cash buyer, sold at auction.

Lender prejudice

Some properties are just difficult to sell, whatever their condition. The problem, once again, lies with the lender. Most lenders have a list of property types on which they will not lend, under any circumstances. Typical among these are ex-local authority flats in a building of more than four or five storeys. They are considered difficult to resell. Then there are flats over certain commercial premises. Typical candidates for immediate exclusion are flats over restaurants, take-aways and hairdressing salons. The reason? Long opening hours and smells! Again, they are considered difficult to resell.

Other lender issues

Lenders will sometimes make a mortgage offer on a property, but subject to substantial, often expensive, works being carried out before the full mortgage amount is released (a retention). This could be because the bathroom needs to be replaced or central heating installed. The cost and the hassle involved may be enough to deter most potential buyers, once they have received the lender's valuation and conditions. After several failed attempts to sell, these properties often go to auction.

TENANTS

Properties with tenants in place do not necessarily pose a problem when it comes to selling. After all, the owner can wait for assured shorthold tenancies to expire or sell to an investor looking for a tenanted property. There are some tenants, however, who *do* pose a problem.

Regulated tenants

A tenant whose tenancy began before the Housing Act 1988 was implemented is a regulated tenant. He has total security of tenure. His very presence slashes the value of the property.

Assured tenants

An assured tenancy (a product of the 1988 Act) offers more security than an assured shorthold tenancy (AST). The fact that the term of the tenancy has expired does not mean that possession can be automatically or easily obtained. The accelerated possession procedure (see Chapter 26) does *not* apply. In the event of a dispute, the matter will be decided by a judge because a court order is required to evict the tenant. There is no certainty as to the outcome. There is the further peculiarity that the tenancy can be passed on to a spouse or partner, on death. Until the rules were changed on 28 February 1997, a great many assured tenancies were created by default. Before that time a tenancy was assumed to be an assured tenancy unless the landlord expressly stated beforehand that it was to be an assured shorthold tenancy. Properties with assured tenancies that have become problems often end up in auctions.

Problem tenants

Even if the correct AST agreement is in place, it may still be difficult and time consuming to deal with problem tenants. The accelerated possession procedure applies only when the fixed term of an AST has expired. It cannot be used to gain quick possession in the course of a tenancy if, for example, a tenant disturbs his neighbours or doesn't pay his rent. The time and the expense of court proceedings in such a case may seem too much, particularly if the tenancy has a long time to run (perhaps most of a 12-month contract!).

THE BASICS

Property auctions are much the same throughout the country and offer much the same service for vendors and buyers.

Locating an auction

By far the quickest way to find a property auction is to begin with the Internet. A simple Google search, for example, under 'property auctions UK' will throw up a number of auction houses you can contact directly, along with a wide variety of auction property databases and newsletters. These are, in effect, simple compilations of auction information collected from auction catalogues throughout the country. You will be asked to subscribe to the publication in order to get the information.

The catalogue

Every auction house produces a catalogue many weeks before the auction. This contains details of all properties to be included in the auction sale and you must get a copy. There are, however, two points to bear in mind about the catalogue entries:

- The fact that there is an entry for a property does not guarantee that the property will be there on the day of the auction. Offers can be made privately beforehand and the property can be withdrawn. It is important to check with the auction house before deciding to bid.

- Ignore the guide price. You must be prepared to pay considerably more than this. Check with the local estate agents for more realistic price levels.

Legal pack

Because an auction sale is an instant and binding contract, everyone entering a property at auction must supply a legal pack prepared by their solicitor. This is then made available *before* the auction to prospective bidders. It will contain copies of title deeds, search results, leases, etc., and is essential reading for your solicitor before you contemplate bidding for the property. If you make a successful bid without obtaining or reading the legal pack, you are *still* contractually bound to complete.

Viewing

To view, arrange surveys, etc., you will normally have one of two possibilities – contact the auction house directly or, more commonly, contact the estate agent acting for the auction house. Where no agent is involved auction houses usually arrange viewing days when anyone can turn up at the property between certain times.

Fees

Apart from the price charged for the catalogue and legal pack there are normally no further costs for the buyer. For the vendor, however, it is a different matter. There is a fee (anything from

£250 upwards, depending on the size of the catalogue display) for having the property included in the auction catalogue. This, however, is the least of their problems! The real cost is the percentage fee based on the ultimate price paid. This is normally 2–2.5%. But expect an additional 0.5% if an estate agent is also appointed to take inquiries. The overall cost could therefore be considerably higher than selling through an estate agent.

PREPARING FOR AUCTION

The auction itself is the simplest part of the process. When the hammer falls the property is sold and both sides are committed. The purchaser immediately provides a 10% deposit in cash (or bank draft) and must pay the balance within 28 days. The tricky part, however, is the preparation for the auction.

Surveys

When purchasing in the normal way it is difficult to avoid a survey of some sort. This is because the mortgage lender will insist on one. While this is called a valuation (and does not entail a nuts-and-bolts examination of the property), it will highlight any major problems that need to be addressed. On the basis of this report the lender will decide whether or not to lend and on what conditions. Many buyers will go further and commission a full structural survey or a homebuyer's report (not as extensive as a full structural and not as expensive) before deciding to proceed. When it comes to auction properties the need for a survey is even greater, and it would be foolhardy in the extreme not to commission one. This has obvious implications in terms of cost, time constraints and the ultimate outcome:

◆ Surveys are not cheap.

◆ There must be adequate time to carry out the survey before the auction.

◆ The outlay is wasted if you fail to buy the property.

Cost of repairs

More often than not, the survey will highlight a number of problems with the property. The cost of any essential repairs or alterations will have to be calculated and taken into account when deciding the maximum bid to make for the property. At least two estimates should be obtained for the work from local builders.

Legal work

While a solicitor is needed for any purchase of property, his role in an auction purchase can be more important than usual. Do neighbours have a right of way over the property? Are there restrictive covenants on the property? Has the local council given Tesco permission to build at the bottom of your garden? If leasehold, does the lease allow you to sublet? Is the title sound? You will need answers to these questions *before* you bid. Some legal information may be contained in the auctioneer's information pack. Your solicitor will need to check this also. A solicitor must, therefore, be instructed well in advance and must complete his work on time. As with the surveyor, the solicitor will have to be paid regardless of the outcome. More money lost if your bid is not successful!

Mortgage

If you don't have the ready cash for the purchase you will have to raise a mortgage. The only safe course of action is to arrange this in advance of the auction. But we have already seen what is involved in this process and the time it can take to satisfy a lender (see Chapter 10). No lender will make an offer on a property without a valuation (at your expense) and a full investigation of your own circumstances. It is not a fast process. For this reason many people settle for the quicker option of a decision in principle (see Chapter 10). This falls well short of a full mortgage offer and is little more than a credit check, based on the following information:

- Name and address.
- Income.
- Price of property (your maximum bid).
- Mortgage required.
- Estimated rent from the property (if buy-to-let).

What you will know from this process is that you, yourself, under certain circumstances, are an acceptable risk to a lender. This does **not**, however, mean that a mortgage is guaranteed. Two things will still be required – a satisfactory valuation of the property (together with a satisfactory rental assessment) and documentary evidence of your own financial position. In other words, it could all still go pear-shaped!

A full mortgage offer is clearly preferable. But how can this be achieved in the limited time available before the auction? The answer, sadly, is with great difficulty. The problem is that many centralised, buy-to-let (BTL) lenders will not value an auction property. Since they know that few cases will go to completion they are simply providing work for valuers and involving their admin staff in fruitless activities. Your own bank, however, can have greater flexibility in such matters and, since they already know your financial background, are likely to be considerably more helpful. In such circumstances a valuation can be carried out promptly and a formal mortgage offer made as soon as you have made a successful bid. There is then every possibility that completion can take place before the 28-day period has expired.

How to calculate the maximum bid

There is naturally a limit to what you will pay for the property of your choice. When buying in the normal way it is easy enough to recognise this limit and to stick to it. If a foolishly high offer has been made there is plenty of time before exchange of contracts to repent and withdraw it. At an auction there is no such luxury. When the gavel falls the property is yours. The matter is complicated further by the fact that most auction purchases are far from simple. Many will involve additional expenditure on repairs or major works. All the following should be considered when arriving at your maximum bid.

Guide price
The auction catalogue will contain a guide price for each property to be auctioned. Ignore it! At best, treat it as a minimum figure. Most properties sell for a great deal more than the guide price, which is there largely to attract unsuspecting bidders.

Repair costs
See above.

Survey and legal costs
See above.

Stamp Duty Land Tax (SDLT)
SDLT at anything from 1% to 4% of the purchase price is a very

serious consideration. Your solicitor will be asking for it when you pay the balance of the price.

Mortgage costs
Lenders' arrangement fees are often added to the loan and will not impact on your cashflow at the outset. Brokers' fees, however, are not and these can be as high as SDLT. If you feel you have to use a broker, factor in his costs.

Bridging loan costs
If you are unfortunate enough to require one of these, the impact could be so great that any savings by buying at auction could be wiped out (see Chapter 11 for possible costs). Factor these in if you are a likely candidate for such a loan.

The deposit
Having decided the absolute maximum you will pay for the property, you now have to consider the possibility that you may succeed in buying it! If you are successful in your bid, you will need to pay a 10% deposit, in cash, on the spot. You cannot arrive empty handed at the auction. As it would not be advisable to turn up with a briefcase full of used fivers, you will need to arrange a cash equivalent form of payment. A bank or building society draft (sometimes called a bank or building society cheque) is the same as cash. It does, however, need to be prepared in advance by the bank or building society. To this end you will need to know two things – the name of the payee and the amount. Check with the auction house for the former and use your maximum bid (see above) for the latter. This will also have the desirable effect of discouraging you from exceeding your maximum bid! If you are fortunate enough to buy for less than your maximum, you will be reimbursed the difference.

Acclimatise yourself

If you have never been to an auction before you should attend a few, just to observe. Accustom yourself to the auctioneer's jargon, the speed of the bidding, the rate at which the bidding increases (£1,000, £5,000, £10,000) and the interaction between auctioneer and bidders.

Proof of ID

Don't set out without a passport or driving licence. If you have a photo licence, bring both parts.

AT THE AUCTION

Get there on time!

Register

If you intend to bid you will have to register as soon as you arrive. Like banks and other financial institutions, auction houses are paranoid about money laundering (what better place to dispose of large sums of drug money than at a property auction!) and, for this reason, will want to establish your identity in a way that will satisfy the authorities. Hence your passport.

Guide price

The auction catalogue offers an indication of the price expected (the guide price). You will soon discover that this bears little relation to the successful bid, which is always higher (see above).

Reserve price

This is the minimum the vendor will accept and the figure will not be revealed. If it is not achieved, the property is withdrawn.

Successful bid

If your bid is successful you will be asked for a driving licence or a passport and contact details for your solicitor or licensed conveyancer. You will then sign a contract – a legally binding contract – and hand over 10%. You have now exchanged contracts and the property is yours. You will be given a memorandum of sale.

AFTER THE AUCTION

What you do now depends on whether you have bought the property or not.

Successful bid

You have to pay the balance within 28 days. You must now find it! If your mortgage has been successfully arranged in advance, there should be no problem. If not, you may need bridging finance until a mortgage is arranged. This is not an instant process! Don't leave matters to the last minute (see Chapter 11). Buildings insurance is required from exchange of contracts (and you have exchanged contracts). You should put cover in place immediately.

Unsuccessful bid

You may have failed for two reasons – the reserve price wasn't achieved or you were outbid. There is nothing you can do if you have been outbid but, in the event of a property remaining unsold, you can always approach the vendor or his agent directly and make an offer.

(18)

New Build or Old?

The temptation to buy new is everywhere. Developers, after all, must shift their stock and they market aggressively to that end. But should you give in to temptation? First, consider the nature of the marketing.

RENTAL GUARANTEES

For two, three or more years the developer will guarantee a rental yield of, say, 6%. In other words, he will pay the rent at this level whether tenants can be found or not.

If the developer is offering rental guarantees on the development he is, by definition, targeting investors like yourself. But this is precisely the sort of development you should avoid at all costs because there will be far too many investors chasing too few tenants. Rents will fall and future investors will stay clear, thus driving down values.

The rental guarantee itself is nothing more than a discount on the price, dressed up as a rental guarantee. But it carries worrying implications:

◆ The developer has clearly overbuilt and is desperate.

◆ Secondly, he has no confidence in the rental market and, if *he* has no confidence, why should you?

◆ Although it is, in reality, a discount on the price, the Inland Revenue will treat it as rental income and tax it accordingly, even if there is no tenant in place!

SLICK MARKETING

When you go along to see a show-flat you will be impressed. After all, it is brand spanking new, tastefully decorated and fully equipped with the latest in furniture and modern conveniences.

You will be given information on how very letable the properties are and what excellent capital growth you can expect. It will also be pointed out that a new property like this requires little maintenance and you can wave good-bye to all those emergency call-out charges you would otherwise expect. But the fact that maintenance costs are likely to be less is neither here nor there, given the vastly greater price you will pay for a new build (see below)!

If you show any interest at this stage you will be instantly introduced to your very own mortgage adviser who will start the mortgage process then and there. There are real dangers here:

◆ The relationship between developer and mortgage adviser is incestuous. Neither can succeed without the other and the pressure to sell is intense.

◆ Predictions of rental yields and capital growth can be far from the truth.

Now consider the following self-evident truths about new-build developments targeted at the buy-to-let (BTL) investor:

◆ The price is always higher – considerably higher – than the equivalent second-hand home. When you buy a new car, you can expect an immediate drop in value as soon as it is on the road. It is much the same with new property. Unlike a car, however, your property may increase in value again, but it will take some time to catch up.

◆ The extra cost of the purchase eats into your yield.

◆ Because of the higher price for the property your mortgage will be higher than it would otherwise be. Any increase in interest rates will be that much more painful for you. Likewise, during any void period, your ongoing mortgage payments could be crippling.

◆ As there is no track record of service charges you don't know what to expect in the years to come. Initial charges will always be low to attract buyers. The hike will come later!

◆ As the development is targeted at BTL investors, few residential purchasers may express an interest. Yet, when you come to sell you will not want to exclude the residential market. Indeed, when you buy you should always bear in mind that you may well depend on the residential market for a sale.

TIP

So what should you do if, despite all this, you really want to buy a flat in that fantastic riverside development? First, make your own checks on likely rental levels and demand. Not all local agents have links with the developer and some may even tell you the truth! Secondly, don't be mesmerised by the rental guarantee. Do your own calculations in the usual way and, if the figures don't stack up, don't buy. Thirdly, check if the builder will roll up the guaranteed rental into a single figure and take it directly off the price. This would have the beneficial effects of avoiding income tax on the sum (see above) and immediately improving your rental yield. Lastly, project yourself forward to the end of the guarantee and ask yourself if you are comfortable with the prospect of letting or selling when that time comes. Trust your instinct.

One final word: professional landlords don't buy new build.

Buying off Plan

Of all the property get-rich-quick schemes to take hold in recent years, buying off plan is in a league of its own. After all, who could resist the following?

- Instant discount!
- Capital growth before you complete!
- No deposit to pay!
- Sell before you buy!
- Join a club to make it easier still!

Too good to be true? Let us consider these claims in some detail.

INSTANT DISCOUNT?

Most off-plan purchases (i.e. where you agree to buy the property before it is constructed) have a built-in discount to attract new customers. A discount is a logical way to achieve this. Ideally the developer will have sold every property before it is built! But what exactly is this discount and can it be relied upon?

In reality the discount has always been available and was part of the developer's financial planning from the outset. Like all marketing strategies, however, it is presented as something very special and just for you! For this reason you will frequently encounter it in advertisements (web based or in newspapers) for property clubs. Clubs of this kind (see below) claim to be able to negotiate discounts for you because they can, in effect, bulk buy. In fact you can negotiate your own discount, in most cases, if you approach the developer or his agent directly. By so doing you will save a great deal of money (see below).

More important than this, however, is the question of the discount itself. Is it real? This raises two issues – the valuation and the role of lenders in the process.

Valuations

Did you ever sell a property? If so, you will undoubtedly have called in two or three local agents to value it. Notice anything? You got two or three completely different valuations! When you finally sold your property, did the price paid bear much relation to any of the valuations you received? What does that tell you?

Basically, there is no science at all to the valuation process. Anyone with any knowledge of the local property market could have put a price on your property and come within spitting distance of any of the valuations you received! Yet your valuers had impressive qualifications – enough letters after their names to make a reasonable alphabet soup!

When it comes to buy-to-let (BTL) valuations, the situation is stranger still. The major BTL lenders use big nationwide valuers. These valuers, in turn, pass the instruction to a 'local office'. But *local* for these valuers never means around the corner from your property. It could cover a swathe of the country from Hertfordshire to northwest London! A valuer from an office in Potters Bar could be sent to value a property in Dollis Hill, London NW2.

When it comes, therefore, to the discount on an off-plan valuation it is sensible to bear in mind that the valuation itself is highly suspect and in the real world might never be realised. A 15% discount on such a valuation is largely meaningless.

The lenders

In a world of property fantasy, mortgage lenders are the nearest we can get to reality. This is because their business is entirely based on the worst possible case scenario – that you, the borrower, might fail to meet your mortgage payments and the lender has to step in to repossess and sell the property. Charming! It does mean, however, that these hard-nosed, faceless people have a keener interest than most in the true value of your property. They may, after all, have to sell it.

So why do so many lenders refuse to accept builders' discounts at all, insisting, instead, on lending on the actual price paid? Why do the small handful that do accept them insist that they be restricted to 10%, with you, the borrower, being required to stump up half of this 10% as part of your deposit? Do they know something we don't? The short answer is yes. The entire builder's discount business is a nonsense and the lenders know it (see Chapter 6)!

CAPITAL GROWTH BEFORE COMPLETION?

As if an initial discount weren't enough, the property is bound to be worth more by the time you complete!

The basis for this assertion is the inevitable time lag between the initial commitment to purchase and the completion of the building itself. This can be one to two years. Prices will certainly have risen by then, won't they? Such a question is aimed at those with very short memories! Buying off plan was all the rage at the end of the 1980s in the UK. The subsequent property crash left off-plan buyers between a rock and a hard place – complete on a property that had collapsed in value or walk away and lose their deposit. Most walked away, vowing never to be taken in again.

Property is a long-term investment, not a short-term gamble.

NO DEPOSIT TO PAY?

Still unsure? If I could show you a way to achieve the property dream of a lifetime without using any of your own money at all, what would you say? Difficult to resist, isn't it? You can be completely penniless and still build a property empire! This claim rests on two premises:

+ That the property will be valued by a lender at 15% more than you will pay for it.

+ That the same lender will then happily waive the 15% deposit they would normally require from you!

This is never-never land! It simply won't happen. All lenders work in the same way. They lend on the valuation or the price, whichever is lower.

In practice this is how the 15% discount works: the lender lends on the valuation and the valuation is the price paid. The lender agrees to a developer's 10% gifted deposit, to be matched by an equal contribution from the buyer. A typical formula is as follows:

Lender   80%
Developer   10%
Buyer   10%

The sale proceeds on this basis with the full, non-discounted price being paid for the property. As the buyer has paid a total of 90% (between mortgage and deposit) instead of 85% (with his 15% discount), the developer rebates 5% on completion (the lender may not be aware of this cash refund or may turn a blind eye to it). It is clear, however, that the buyer has to find at least 10% of his own money immediately and has to wait until completion for a partial refund.

SELL BEFORE YOU COMPLETE?

Unlike share purchase, buying property off plan means buying something that doesn't yet exist. More accurately, you are committing yourself to purchase it when it does exist. As the developer is also committed to selling to you, you have something you can sell on before completion – an agreement to purchase at a set price. In a rising market someone may be willing to buy this from you at a higher price than you have agreed to pay.

A few points are worth making about this intriguing idea:

◆ This is only possible in a rising market. If the market falls, you may be wondering whether to complete on the purchase yourself.

◆ You must complete on your purchase in order to sell on. If you can't for any reason (e.g. failure to get a mortgage), you will suffer the double whammy of losing your deposit and having nothing to sell on at a profit.

◆ If you do sell on at a higher price, you will have an immediate capital gains tax liability and no way of avoiding it. If you wait to complete the purchase, move in (making the property your principal residence) and then sell, you will have no tax to pay because you will benefit from the principal residence tax exemption.

◆ In a rising market you may, in any event, be better advised to complete on the sale and keep the property, even if you don't move in and make the property your main residence. The reason is that the increased value could enable you to drawdown further funds from the lender without incurring any tax liability whatsoever. These funds can be used as deposit money for a further purchase. And it gets even better. These drawdown funds are fully tax deductible!

JOIN A CLUB?

Along with the growth of off-plan marketing comes the inevitable club for off-plan investors. Almost exclusively web based, these clubs offer all the usual 'advantages' of buying off plan, plus the additional benefits of finding the property for you and sorting the mortgage. Just sit back and let them do the work!

You will be issued with a prospectus setting out why you should invest in a property in a planned new development. The club will claim to have researched all areas of importance and will provide analyses on some or all of the following:

◆ Social, commercial and industrial background of the town.
◆ Any planned public sector investment.
◆ Statistics on employment, housing mix, average income.

- Prospects for new employment opportunities.
- Transport and any planned improvements.
- Statistics on rents and prices.
- Prospects for rental demand.
- Details of valuations obtained.

The basis of your relationship with such a club is *trust*. You effectively delegate everything to the club organisers and trust them to deliver. In addition to giving them your trust you will, of course, also give them a lot of money – anything from 2 to 5% of the purchase price as a finder's fee.

The disadvantages of using such clubs are as follows.

Cost
The finder's fee, payable with the 10% deposit on exchange, will seriously erode any savings on the price. In addition, most clubs charge an annual subscription fee.

The development
Such clubs promote individual developments, not individual properties in different locations. To that end they are useful to developers for whom they act, in effect, as estate agents. There are several problems with such an arrangement:

- There are only so many developments planned at any given time. A club in search of one to promote may be tempted to grab what is available rather than what is really suitable. After all, the finder's fee is payable up front, within 28 days of the decision to purchase.

♦ Much, if not all, of the 'research' carried out by such clubs is provided by the developers themselves. There may be little original research involved. Such information is, not surprisingly, slanted heavily towards making the development a very attractive proposition.

♦ Investment clubs have very close relationships with mortgage brokers and lenders. In fact, they tend to have just one mortgage broker who will always use the same lender! While you are free to go elsewhere, it is always made clear at the outset that things will be difficult if you do. On this basis there is no prospect of really independent financial advice. To make matters worse, the mortgage broker will nearly always charge a fee, in addition to the procuration fee they will receive from the lender (see Chapter 9).

♦ By definition, properties bought through a club will tend to come on stream at the same time in the same development. All the eager purchasers will be looking for tenants at the same time!

There is no substitute for doing your own research and taking responsibility for your own decisions. If a development looks particularly interesting, check with local letting agents and get a feel for the real state of the rental market. Check with the local planning department to see if other developments are planned for the same area, virtually guaranteeing a glut of rental properties in the near future. Contact the developer directly and see if a discount can be negotiated. Finally, remember that, if you buy through an investment club, you are buying off plan. If you buy off plan you are buying new. Professional landlords do not buy new.

Part Four

Tenants

(20)

Using Agents

When looking for tenants, especially for the first time, there is a strong temptation to hand the entire business over to a letting agent. After all, they are the professionals, aren't they? Let us consider in detail what you can expect from an agent and just how professional they really are.

FINDING TENANTS

There is no doubt this is a daunting exercise for the first-time landlord. An agent will happily take on this task, undertaking to find the tenants, interview them and take up all necessary references. In practice, how does this work?

The agency agreement

Normally an agent will require you to sign an agreement before undertaking any work on your behalf. While much of this is routine stuff there are some crucial elements to be aware of and guard against. First and foremost there is the agent's fee.

For finding a tenant (as opposed to finding and managing) the fee could be anywhere between 7 and 12%, plus VAT. The important thing to remember is that this fee is negotiable. For finding a tenant only you should not pay more than 7 or 8%.

In addition to negotiating the fee you must establish clearly over what term the fee is based. In other words, will you pay 7% of the rent over a 6-month term or over 12? Not surprisingly, all agents assume a 12-month tenancy agreement and will draw one up without asking. The temptation to go for the longer term is irresistible. As we shall see later, you should never enter into a 12-month tenancy agreement.

The next point is something never raised by the agent and never considered by the landlord – renewals. Hidden in the small print of the agreement is a reference to ongoing commission. If your tenant stays beyond the 6 or 12-months initial period you will pay the agent again and again. Make it clear you will not accept renewal fees under any circumstances. There are plenty of agents who will waive this if asked.

Next, watch out for the hidden sale commission. If your tenant loves your property so much that he subsequently offers to buy it, your agent will be back for a further slice – a fee for selling the property! This could be as high as 2.5% and is buried in the agreement you sign with them. Cross it out, initial it and get the agent to do the same.

To sum up:

◆ Negotiate the fee.
◆ Fee should be based on a 6-month contract only.
◆ Do not accept renewals.
◆ Do not accept a sale commission.
◆ Make sure any agreement you sign is amended accordingly.

The tenants

It is a sad fact that most agents pay little regard to the type of tenant they find. Their primary objective is to fill your empty property and bank their fee. Yet the type of tenant is a crucial decision. Is the area ideal for young professionals or students? Would housing benefit tenants be more appropriate? What type of tenant would best suit the other occupants of the building? Unless you give the agent some idea of what you are looking for, he will interview everyone who walks through his door.

References

Taking up references is something agents always stress as part of their service, as though this could only be carried out by a professional agent. In essence it is simplicity itself (see below), but is frequently carried out by agents in a very careless and haphazard manner. The essential references required are:

- ◆ employer
- ◆ landlord
- ◆ bank
- ◆ credit.

All reference taking should be based on the premise that the prospective tenant is hiding something! Harsh though this may sound, it is the only safe way to proceed. The consequences of getting it wrong at this stage could be disastrous.

For this reason both a written and a verbal reference should be obtained from an employer. The existence of the company should be verified independently through directory enquiries or the telephone directory. In the case of a limited company it is a simple matter to check it out online through the website for Companies' House. Too often the contact details provided by the prospective tenant are accepted without query. When a reference on a company letterhead is received, this should be followed by a phone call to the human resources department for further confirmation. Fake employer references are not uncommon. Most agents, however, consider their work done on receipt of a plausible-looking reference on a company letterhead.

A previous landlord's reference is crucial, but is the easiest of all references to fake. Most agents rely entirely on a verbal reference obtained on the phone. For all they know they could be talking to the tenant's best friend!

In most cases, as we shall see, bank references are of little value. Agents, however, never fail to get them!

A credit reference, through a credit reference agency such as Equifax or Experian, can provide invaluable information about your would-be tenant. Agents never apply for one. The reason is simple. Such reports can often reveal a cavalier attitude, on the applicant's part, to meeting his financial commitments. They can also, as we shall see, reveal a lot worse. The landlord could easily reject the applicant on these grounds alone, thus losing the agent a sale that was otherwise in the bag!

If you decide to use an agent to take up references, you should work on the assumption that you will still have some involvement in the process. Failure to keep a close eye on the proceedings could result in the very consequences you are trying to avoid. At the very least you should:

- insist on a credit check
- obtain copies of all references
- make your own follow-up enquiries on employer and landlord.

MANAGING

In addition to finding a tenant, agents offer a full management service. In this case they will collect the rent and deal with the day-to-day management of the property. Effectively, you hand the whole matter over to them.

There are serious implications for the landlord in such an arrangement. Once again they are tucked away in the small print of the management agreement.

The fee

Typically this can be up to 5% (+ VAT) on top of the finder's fee. It is, however, very negotiable and should never be accepted as read.

Collecting rent

The agent undertakes to collect the rent and pass it on (less his fee) to you. It is, however, never stated exactly how this should be done and it differs greatly from one agent to another.

It is extraordinary how so many agents still require the tenant to call to the office to pay the rent! In the days of universal bank accounts, a standing order should be the only acceptable method of payment. To make matters worse, many agents then send a cheque to the landlord! The effect of such an antiquated system is delay, delay, delay. Under such a system rent can arrive in your bank account two to three weeks after it is due!

Inspections

Most agreements refer to the agent's duty to inspect the property
at regular intervals and report back to the landlord. In practice
such an undertaking is never honoured and you are unlikely ever
to receive a report of any kind! So long as the rent is paid the
agent ceases to care. You will be blissfully unaware of the
condition of the property, how many people are actually living
there or whether the original tenant has long since gone back to
Australia and is now subletting to his mates!

Repairs

One thing agents are very good at is arranging essential repairs. If
the boiler breaks down they have a man who can fix it. What you
don't know is that, in most cases, they receive commission from
the plumber or electrician for getting them the work! For this
reason they will use only one company for all their repairs and
will not obtain alternative quotes. As a result, repair bills go
through the roof.

Agents, tenants and the landlord

When an agent manages a property there are important
implications for the landlord/tenant relationship. In effect there is
no relationship at all, and this has two consequences:

◆ A tenant's attitude to an agent is quite different from his
   attitude to a landlord. A tenant knows that the agent does not
   own the property and never inspects it. So long as the rent is
   paid, he will not expect trouble from the agent. As a result the
   tenant will feel free to behave in a manner a hands-on landlord
   might find entirely unacceptable.

◆ A difficult or unresponsive agent can lose a landlord good tenants. Some agents treat their tenants with ill-disguised contempt, failing to deal with their problems or take them seriously. As the tenant has no contact with the landlord, the latter remains entirely oblivious to this state of affairs.

Ending management agreement

If a landlord decides to terminate his management agreement with a letting agent, he may be in for a rude shock when the tenancy agreement is up for renewal. The landlord will get a bill from the agent for another year's fee! Although he is no longer managing the property, the agent will demand an ongoing finder's fee if the original tenant remains in the property.

The deposit

The question of who should hold the tenant's deposit has always been a contentious issue. When an agent manages a property, however, they always assume that they should hold the deposit. In reality, as they keep the interest earned on this money, it is simply another source of income. The real danger, however, is that the deposit will disappear altogether, should the agent go out of business. In such a situation the landlord is legally obliged to replace it! The landlord remains ultimately responsible.

The Housing Act 2004 has improved matters greatly in respect of deposits and the rights of both landlords and tenants in this regard (see Chapter 25). Where an agent is used, however, it is still best practice for the landlord to deal with the deposit himself and not trust the agent to comply correctly with the legislation. If everything goes pear-shaped it is the landlord, not the agent, who carries the can.

Tax

It is not generally known (and agents certainly don't volunteer the information) that the Inland Revenue routinely requires agents to provide them with details of landlords and properties on their books. Letting agents, in turn, are not obliged to inform their landlords that they have provided this information to the taxman. Naturally, they don't.

If you decide to instruct an agent to manage your properties, you should do all the following:

◆ Negotiate a reduction in the fee.

◆ Insist that the rent is paid by standing order to the agent and paid directly into *your* bank account by the agent *on the same day*. If the agent cannot provide this service, go elsewhere.

◆ Insist on a commitment to providing inspection reports at specified times and remember to ask for them when they don't arrive.

◆ For repairs, always ask for a second quote. If one isn't provided, get one yourself. In this way you will build up a bank of local contacts and greatly reduce your repair bills.

◆ Make it clear that, in the event of the management agreement being terminated, there is no ongoing financial commitment to the agent. The agreement should be altered to reflect this.

◆ On no account allow the agent to hold the deposit.

◆ Tell the agent you wish to be advised if your details are passed to the Inland Revenue or any other agency. The agreement should be altered to reflect this.

DIY

The alternative to using an agent is to do it yourself – find the tenants and manage the property. Horrified at the prospect? No need to be. It is far simpler than letting agents would have you believe.

PREPARING THE PROPERTY

Before embarking on the quest for tenants, it is worth asking if your property is ready for them! Initial impressions are crucial and some basic dos and don'ts need to be observed.

It is a very long time since any prospective tenant would gratefully accept anything on offer. The market for rented accommodation is now highly competitive, and failing to meet a tenant's reasonable expectations on a first viewing can be fatal. So what is now on most tenants' wish list?

Neutral decor

Magnolia walls, white ceilings and a neutral carpet, if you must have one (see below). Any deviation from this formula is a serious risk you will live to regret.

A washer/dryer

Hanging clothes over the bath-tub is no longer acceptable.

Laminate flooring

This has become a near obsession. Don't fight it. In most cases it is cheaper to put down than carpet and it will last a good deal longer. One word of caution, however. If there is an apartment underneath yours, check there is adequate sound insulation between the floors. Most conversions, for example, will have no insulation at all and your tenants will sound like a herd of elephants! Life for your neighbour can become a nightmare, with dire consequences for your tenants and yourself.

Water pressure

The shower is of crucial importance for busy people and your tenant will want plenty of power. If the water pressure is low, install a power shower.

A dishwasher

Not yet a deal breaker but becoming increasingly desirable as all new-build, purpose-built apartment blocks provide them as standard. If you can find the space, install one.

Clean and tidy

This may sound blindingly obvious but, if the property is still occupied by outgoing tenants when a prospective tenant comes to view, it will *not* look clean and tidy. No attempt should be made to market a property until the existing tenants have left.

FINDING TENANTS

Now that all is ready, where to look for tenants?

The Internet

In recent years the Internet has made life a great deal easier for both tenant and landlord. Many sites are now aimed specifically at particular tenant groups, such as students. A website like www.accommodationforstudents.com will provide all that is needed to secure the right tenant, at a reasonable cost, in a reasonable time. Apart from such specialist sites there are a great many general property letting sites. Check out, for example, www.fish4homes.co.uk, www.lettingzone.com or www.gumtree.com. All sites have a 'Wanted' section where you could find the right tenant without needing to advertise at all. A few key words on a search engine such as Google will reveal many more.

University accommodation

If students are your market there is also the accommodation department of the university you are targeting. Most universities charge nothing to add your property details to their student accommodation website and their housing lists. Every year, usually in March, these lists are distributed at the fresher fairs. Accommodation departments will, however, have certain requirements that need to be fulfilled before your property is accepted. In most cases an up-to-date gas safety certificate and an electrical safety certificate (originals, not copies) will suffice. Always ask for a copy of the full housing list both to check that your property is correctly advertised and to see what the competition is offering.

Newspapers

With more and more people using the web to search for properties, newspapers increasingly play a secondary and more expensive role. They do, however, have a place when all else fails. For London and the south east, the property section of *LOOT* remains the firm favourite and has the advantage of a web version in addition to the paper. Adverts can be placed using the website www.LOOT.com or by phone (usually a lot easier!). Elsewhere in the country there isn't a simple, dedicated publication like this available, so it is a matter of trial and error, using the classified section of local and national papers.

In all cases it is important to add the words 'NO AGENTS' at the end of your advert. If you don't do this you will be inundated with calls from letting agents offering to find a tenant for you! They will assure you they can get a higher rent than you are looking for, the difference to be paid to them as their fee. If you accept such an offer you will be faced with two problems:

◆ People who go to agents in search of accommodation also read papers! You and the agent could both find the same tenant – a recipe for embarrassment and confusion.

◆ If you have pitched your rental figure correctly, the agent will not succeed in getting a higher figure. He will meet with repeated resistance, prolonging the whole business unnecessarily. It is best to avoid such arrangements altogether.

INITIAL CONTACT

When showing prospective tenants around your property, try to get *all* interested parties to come *at the same time*. If you have an apartment for two, for example, don't arrange an appointment for one of the two. The person who views the property will report back to his partner, who will find one reason or another to turn it down. It is simply an inefficient way of letting your property and is an incredible time waster for the landlord. If all concerned cannot turn up at a suggested time, ask them to let you know when they can. If they are really interested they will make the effort.

INTERVIEWS AND REFERENCES

Before agreeing to let your property to anyone it is essential to know your tenant. The first step, therefore, when a serious interest is expressed, is to gather essential information. A tenant's information form should be completed. This should contain all the following:

- Name and current address.
- Three-year address history.
- Date of birth.
- Passport number.
- Work, home and mobile numbers.
- Current landlord with address and phone number.
- Details of any state benefits being received.
- Employer's address and phone number.
- Time with employer.
- Three-year employment history.
- Bank address, account number and sort code.
- Personal character referee with address and phone number.
- Signed and dated statement, giving the landlord permission to carry out credit and reference checks.

You can draft a simple form yourself or download a ready-made version from www.landlordzone.co.uk. In addition, you should ask to see three months' bank statements (see below).

This may seem very intrusive but it is no more than a bank or a mortgage lender would require before advancing a loan. Just like a lender, you need assurances that this person (someone, after all, you have never clapped eyes on before) is all he claims to be and can meet the financial commitment he is about to undertake.

Unlike a letting agent you have every reason to check these details thoroughly and have nothing to fear from the results of your inquiries. In particular, the results of a credit check could prove very helpful. Apart from showing how current financial commitments are met, a credit file can show any defaults there may have been and any county court judgments (CCJs) lodged against the applicant. These represent very serious credit problems resulting in intervention by the lender, who has failed to get payment in any other way. The file will also show if the default or CCJ is still unsatisfied. For the landlord, alarm bells should be ringing. A full credit file can be obtained through the credit reference agencies Equifax or Experian. A simplified report can be obtained through the Residential Landlords' Association (RLA) at modest cost.

An employer's reference should be on company letterhead and should indicate:

◆ job title
◆ whether full or part time
◆ length of service and salary.

A follow-up phone call is essential. It goes without saying that the company (if a limited company or PLC) should be checked out on Companies' House website. If it is not a limited company, you might at least expect an entry in the telephone directory.

A bank reference will involve a cost to your prospective tenant (typically £7–£10), and you may ask yourself whether it is really worth while. Most references are so general they are almost useless. Occasionally you will find a bank that tries to be a little more precise, providing, for example, a set of tick-boxed statements such as: 'The customer has a satisfactory record with us of meeting commitments and should be good for your inquiry' or 'The proposed commitment seems high. We do not think our customers should take on a commitment unless it could be met.'

On the whole, however, you may find it more useful to cast your eye over the applicant's last three months' bank statements (originals, of course). You can see, at a glance, whether the account is conducted satisfactorily, whether outgoings regularly exceed income, whether unauthorised overdraft charges have been applied, etc. This is far more informative than most bank references.

A landlord's reference is very important but the easiest of all to fabricate. Agents will happily settle for a name and a phone number (provided by the tenant) and accept any old rubbish they are offered by way of a verbal reference. The last thing they want to do is probe further into the matter! But ask yourself this question: if your applicant has had a bad track record with a landlord, will he provide you with his contact details? Not likely! He will give you the name and phone number of his or her best mate!

The solution is to treat the previous landlord exactly as you treat your prospective tenant – with suspicion. Instead of relying on a phone call, send the landlord a simple form with a few tick-boxes and a stamped addressed envelope. You cannot expect the landlord to write an essay, but a few tick-boxes with headings such as 'Always paid rent on time' or 'Very satisfactory tenant' or 'Would not recommend him/her as a tenant' should not be too onerous. Leave a blank space for comments (you might be lucky). If you don't get a reply, make the phone call, ask about the tenant. Then ask for the form to be returned. Finally, do a simple search in the Land Registry to establish if the landlord owns the property in question. This is not a perfect or foolproof method but it is far more than any agent would do on your behalf.

For the ultra-cautious landlord, there are various rental guarantee insurance schemes. These effectively protect you against the possibility of a defaulting tenant, provided the tenant is selected in a particular way (a credit check, for example, is a routine requirement). All this, of course, in return for a hefty insurance premium (see 'Useful addresses').

What Tenants?

Letting agents frequently claim to have young professionals looking for property to rent. The implication here is that this category of tenant is preferable to any other. This is, of course, complete nonsense. Tenants are people who are either in work or not, honest or not, reliable or not. Their educational or social background has nothing to do with it. A hotel or restaurant chef will never be out of work, whatever the state of the economy. This cannot be said of all young professionals!

Another category of tenant, much vaunted by letting agents, is the 'young executive'. This rare species of tenant, we are to believe, is to be found lurking around building sites waiting for the new luxury apartments to be completed so that he can snap one up to rent (not to buy, you will notice, but to rent). Builders and estate agents are very aware of the importance of this message. It is, after all, only very well paid young executives who will have the cash to pay the huge rents required to service the cost of buying these apartments! The reality, however, is very different. The major cities of the UK are full of brand-new, and very empty, apartments waiting in vain for rich young executives to call. But it could get worse. If the economy takes a tumble and City bonuses shrink, the young executive willing to pay sky-high rents will become an endangered species.

Apart from reminding us that we should not believe the blandishments of agents and should never buy new build, what does all this tell us? Simply that there is no perfect category of tenant to look for and certainly no professional or educational background that should be favoured over any other.

There are, however, certain categories of tenant that are, in one way or another, outside the norm. These are:

* students
* housing benefit tenants
* councils and housing associations
* company lets
* houses of multiple occupation
* tenants in place at time of purchase.

Each presents certain issues for the landlord, and particular care needs to be taken when letting property to such tenants.

STUDENTS

The advantages of owning a student house are considerable.

Yield

Higher-than-average yield (see Chapter 13).

The demand

Provided you have chosen the location carefully and are offering good value for money, you can reasonably expect regular demand for your property. With successive governments encouraging more and more children to go on to university, the demand for private sector accommodation is set to continue for some time.

The foreign student factor

Universities have a strong incentive to attract foreign (i.e. non-EU) students, as the fees paid by these students are, typically, three or four times those paid by UK or EU students. As foreign students tend to be very well funded, there is little risk for the landlord. Indeed, many landlords find foreign students a good deal more reliable than their UK counterparts!

The postgraduate market

Postgraduates lead a very different life from undergraduates. Apart from being more mature and better behaved(!), they work to a 12-month calendar. Prolonged summer holidays are a thing of the past. Summer months are spent in the library, not the flesh-pots of Faliraki. As a result they rent property over a 12-month period, thus avoiding the dead months of July and August – months undergraduates are unwilling to pay for (see below). Postgraduates also tend to be more successful at finding replacements when they leave, thus minimising the annual angst that accompanies the search for new students.

Problems with student lettings

Of the problems associated with student letting, the following are the most common.

Finding new tenants

Great care needs to be taken to get the timing of any advertising campaign right. If you miss the house-hunting frenzy that accompanies the distribution of the housing lists, you may have great trouble filling your house. The reason is that this is normally the only time when students hunt in packs. If you need five students, for example, this is your chance to get all five at once. Later in the year it is often a case of individual students looking for a room. This will make a joint tenancy agreement impossible and cause all sorts of logistical problems. As they will arrive and leave at different times, how are bills to be shared? If one leaves early, how do you find a replacement?

The summer discount problem
As undergraduates have no reason to be around in July and August it is common in many university towns for students to pay a retainer of one month's rent for this period. In effect this means that the property is let for 11 of the 12 months. This problem doesn't arise with postgraduates.

Houses of Multiple Occupation (HMOs)
Student houses will always be houses of multiple occupation (HMOs) (see below).

Student letting: summary
Check when the university housing lists are distributed and make sure your property is on them. Make sure the property is well presented and has all the necessary facilities. If you are accommodating more than three students, for example, a second WC and shower are essential. Students will no longer settle for inferior accommodation.

Try the postgraduate market first. Don't attempt a mixed household of undergraduates and postgraduates. They occupy different worlds and don't want to live together. If you are letting to undergraduates, look for second years (first years are usually in halls of residence). They will have two years to go and may stay with you for both. You will appreciate this when the annual student-hunting season starts and *you* can put your feet up!

Insist on a *joint* tenancy agreement. Set up individual standing orders either from the students' bank accounts or, better still, from their parents'. Choose a spokesperson for the group and liaise with him or her. It makes life a great deal easier.

Obtain contact details for parents and get in touch to introduce yourself. If anything goes wrong you will be looking to the parents to sort it out. Ask the parents to sign a rental guarantee. This should be sent directly to the parents (with a stamped, addressed envelope) and not given to the students to pass on. The guarantee essentially means that the parents will pay any outstanding rent and cover the cost of any damage caused by their offspring. The guarantee form is a legal document and must be correctly drafted. For this reason an up-to-date version should be obtained from one of the recognised landlord organisations such as the Residential Landlords' Association (see 'Useful addresses'). As the parents are guaranteeing the rent, you should consider taking up references on them. If, for example, a parent is unemployed and in receipt of state benefits, your guarantee is largely worthless.

Full-time students are exempt from council tax. Each council, however, has its own requirements for establishing the students' tax-free status (usually the university provides the student with a council tax exemption certificate). It is essential to contact the council and check what their requirements are. If they don't know the property is occupied by students, they will bill *you* for the council tax.

HOUSING BENEFIT TENANTS

Housing benefit is a means of helping people pay their rent at a time when they have little disposable income. It is administered by

the local council on behalf of the Department for Work and
Pensions.

Having the rent paid by the local council has a certain appeal,
and some landlords specialise in housing benefit tenants. Such
tenants can also be very reliable and may occupy the property for
a long time. There are, however, some serious drawbacks that
should be taken into account.

How the rent is paid

The principal attraction for the landlord has been that the rent
was paid directly to him every four weeks, thus removing
altogether the necessity of collecting the rent from the tenant. This
is no longer the case. Since housing benefit was replaced by the
new 'Local housing allowance' (LHA) in 2006, the rent must be
paid to the tenant. The tenant can no longer choose to have the
rent paid directly to the landlord. Only if the tenant is eight weeks
or more in arrears can the landlord apply to the council to have
the rent paid to him. The only other circumstances where this
might occur will be if the tenant is deemed by the council to be
vulnerable.

There is one slight benefit to the landlord in this arrangement.
When rent is paid directly to the landlord, the council has the
right to claw it back if it discovers that the tenant was not entitled
to have it! If the tenant is paid directly, this will not happen.
Most landlords, however, will find this poor consolation indeed.

Deposit

By definition, tenants on very low income are not likely to have a
damage deposit. Some councils operate a deposit scheme that

guarantees payment if the tenant leaves owing rent, or if damage has been done. Not all councils, however, have such a scheme.

Rent paid in arrears
As if that weren't bad enough, the rent is paid in arrears – normally four weeks in arrears.

Rent level
With the replacement of housing benefit by LHA, there is a new system of calculating the rent that a tenant will qualify for. Instead of basing the calculation on the actual property that the tenant wants to rent, the rent officers will determine the average rent for this type of property in the area and use that instead. Landlords with better-than-average properties will not benefit from this change.

Regardless of the method of calculating the rent allowance, it will rarely cover the whole rent. The tenant must find the difference and the landlord must collect it. A market rent is difficult to achieve.

Get-rich-quick schemes
The whole housing benefit system has spawned a plethora of get-rich schemes based on the premise that housing benefit rental income will simply pour in, thanks to the munificence of Her Majesty's Government! Let us consider what is on offer here.

Typically, a local estate agent or property company in the Midlands or the north of England will buy up a few streets of boarded-up, abandoned houses in an entirely run-down area. They may have paid as little as £5,000 per house. For a similar sum, they will do these up and sell them on for, say, £25,000. A tidy profit. As nobody would buy such properties under normal circumstances they are marketed as hassle-free income generators with yields as high as 15%. The income comes from (you've guessed it) housing benefit. There is an undertaking to find suitable housing benefit tenants for you after the purchase, with a rental guarantee (for a fee) to provide additional security. Mortgages are arranged (for a fee). The vendors will also offer (for a fee) to manage the properties, thus leaving the purchaser with nothing at all to do (apart from paying all the fees). So, what can go wrong?

♦ Several such schemes have been shown to be scams and the companies involved have been closed down by the Department for Trade and Industry. In some cases the properties were not in a fit state to be occupied. In others no attempt was made to find any tenants and the rental guarantees proved useless (such insurance schemes only pay out if attempts have been made to find tenants!). To make matters worse, when properties are left unoccupied for a protracted period, the buildings insurance cover is no longer valid.

♦ If all goes well and the house is tenanted with housing benefit tenants there is little prospect of capital growth. These properties are simply not in sought-after areas and are only ever likely to appeal to other investors, thus severely restricting resale options. This appeal may now itself be in doubt, following the changes to housing benefit rules.

♦ The change likely to have the greatest impact is the switch from payment to landlord to payment to tenant. Anyone with a portfolio of such properties will be in for a bumpy ride.

- The change in the rental calculation may also have an effect. Where, in the past, the housing benefit may have covered the whole rent, it may now not do so. Rents may have to fall to whatever average rent the local rent officers set.

- The real beneficiaries of such schemes are the vendors and estate agents who market them. Substantial profits are made on the sale, additional fees are paid at various stages along the way and there is a healthy income stream from the ongoing management fees after the sale. It is certainly a case of get rich quick – but not for the purchaser!

COUNCILS/HOUSING ASSOCIATIONS

An alternative to letting property in the usual way is to hand it over completely to a local council or housing association. In this case a lease is granted to the council or housing association whose officers find the tenants and manage the property. The landlord has no direct involvement. The essential features of such schemes are as follows:

- The owner signs a lease for three or five years.

- Tenants are provided by the council or housing association.

- Responsibility for managing the property passes to the council or housing association.

- An agreed rent is paid to the owner, whether the property is occupied or not.

- The property is normally expected to be unfurnished, with the possible exception of cooker and fridge/freezer.

◆ The owner will still be responsible for essential repairs and maintenance and for gas and electricity certificates.

◆ At the end of the lease the owner is guaranteed the return of the property in the same condition as when it was handed over.

The attraction of this arrangement to the property owner is obvious. He can effectively wave goodbye to most landlord headaches, including the inevitable voids and the hassle of finding new tenants. There are, however, some drawbacks:

◆ The choice of tenant is entirely in the hands of the council or housing association. The possibility of neighbours being upset should not be ignored.

◆ Most councils claim to offer a market rent. In reality it is always less. However, if you normally use an agent to find tenants, you will not incur this cost.

◆ Most buy-to-let lenders will not entertain this arrangement as it restricts their right to repossess the property. Strictly speaking, the lender needs to be told in advance of any such agreement. It goes without saying that the property insurer also needs to be advised.

◆ The few lenders who will accept this arrangement draw the line at a three-year lease. If a five-year lease has been entered into, it may prove impossible to remortgage the property during the course of the lease.

COMPANY LETS
Letting property to a limited company is entirely different from

letting it to an individual. It is a *commercial* transaction. Assured shorthold tenancy agreements cannot be used. Instead, a company let agreement needs to be used and this, in turn, needs to be very carefully drafted. The relevant legislation is the Law of Property Act 1925. The essential elements of this agreement are as follows:

♦ A clear statement that the forfeiture provisions of the Law of Property Act 1925 are to apply to the contract.

♦ The parties to the agreement.

♦ The names of the individual or individuals who will occupy the property and the statement that no one else will be allowed to do so.

♦ The term.

♦ The rent.

♦ The deposit and whether interest is to be paid on it.

♦ A provision that, in the event of the company going into liquidation or the tenant becoming bankrupt, the tenancy will end.

♦ List of duties and responsibilities for tenant and landlord.

The following points should be noted:

♦ As the correct wording is essential in this document you should always use an up-to-date version available from one of the national landlord associations.

♦ Before agreeing to a company let, check out the company itself at Companies' House. It is simple and cheap to do this online at www.companieshouse.gov.uk.

HOUSES OF MULTIPLE OCCUPATION (HMOs)

The Housing Act 2004 (in force from 6 April 2006) brings in a number of significant measures that have a direct impact on the residential rental market. The most important of these are the changes relating to the treatment of houses of multiple occupation (HMOs).

HMOs have always existed and local authorities have always had measures for dealing with and registering them. There has, however, been no uniformity either as to the definition of a HMO or under what circumstances a local council should step in and monitor them. The Housing Act changes all that. There is no longer any uncertainty about what exactly constitutes a HMO and there is now in place a mandatory system for licensing. Landlords of HMOs need to be fully aware of how the Act affects them.

Definition of HMO

An HMO is defined by the Act as a building or part of a building (e.g. a flat):

♦ which is occupied by more than one household and in which more than one household shares an amenity (or the building lacks an amenity) such as a bathroom, toilet or cooking facilities, *or*

◆ which is occupied by more than one household and which is a converted building which does not entirely comprise self-contained flats (whether or not there is also a sharing or lack of amenities), *or*

◆ which consists entirely of converted self-contained flats and the standard of conversion does not meet, at a minimum, that required by the 1991 Building Regulation *and* more than one third of the flats are occupied under short tenancies

◆ *and* is 'occupied' by more than one household:
 – as their only or main residence, *or*
 – as a refuge by persons escaping domestic violence, *or*
 – during term time by students, *or*
 – for some other purpose that is prescribed in regulations and the households comprise families (including foster children, children being cared for) and current domestic employees, single persons, cohabiting couples (whether or not of the opposite sex).

As can be seen from the above, the scope of the definition is very wide indeed and will cover many situations quite commonplace in the rental market. For example, it can cover both houses and flats and will definitely cover all student houses with two or more tenants.

So, how will this affect landlords? This will depend largely on whether the property in question needs to be licensed.

Licensing

The Act makes certain HMOs subject to mandatory licensing (licences are granted for five years). In other words, local authorities will have no choice in the matter. They will have to license the property and landlords will have a *duty* to inform the council that they have such a property. Properties subject to mandatory licensing are properties that have:

♦ three or more storeys (the term 'storey' will include any attic or basement which is used or capable of being used for residential purposes)

♦ *and* are occupied by five or more persons

♦ who comprise two or more households.

For compulsory licensing to apply, all three elements of the above must be in place. It follows that not all properties, by any means, will need to be licensed.

The fly in the ointment here, however, is the additional discretionary power given by the Act to local councils to license other categories of property, if they feel it necessary, in order to address certain local issues. This may have the potential to cause problems for landlords in certain parts of the country. A local council could, for example, attempt to deal with anti-social behaviour in a particular area by licensing all rented properties in the area, regardless of size. It is not a decision, however, which the local authority can make on its own. There must first be local consultation with all interested groups and an application must be made to the Secretary of State. The exception to this is where the council in question is deemed to be 'excellent' or 'good'. In this case an application will not be necessary.

In addition to these discretionary powers, some councils have even wider scope for extending their control. These are the councils that operated their own system of HMO registration *before* the new licensing system was introduced in 2006. Where such councils had previously required licences for small HMOs (i.e. less than three storeys and fewer than five tenants) they could continue to require licences for them, if they deemed it necessary to do so.

Exemptions from HMO

Certain properties are specifically excluded from HMO status and are not covered by the Act. Examples are student halls of residence and care homes. Of specific interest to private landlords, however, are the following:

◆ Buildings occupied by a resident landlord with up to two tenants.

◆ Buildings, or parts of buildings, occupied by no more than two households, each of which is a single person (i.e. two one-person flat shares).

Effect of licensing

The landlord of a licensed HMO will certainly notice the difference. The first shock of many is the cost. The local authority will charge a licensing fee. There is no cap on this fee and each council can set its own rate. Then comes the mandatory inspection of gas and electrical appliances, furniture and smoke alarms. In addition the council can decide to take into account tenant behaviour and landlord (or agent) management. They can insist that specific works be carried out.

And it doesn't end there! The Act provides for severe penalties for non-compliance. A fine of £20,000 can be levied for exceeding the number of tenants allowed under the licence or for failing to obtain a licence in the first place. Rent received during the unlicensed period will have to be returned. Failure to carry out specified works or alterations can result in a £5,000 fine and revoking of the licence.

In extreme cases the council can step in and take over the management of the property, either on an interim basis (for 12 months) or a full basis (five years). During this time they can perform pretty well all the functions of the landlord, such as carrying out repairs, collecting the rent and finding new tenants. As for the landlord, all he is entitled to after all this is any surplus cash the council's property managers may have left over!

Other HMO headaches

Whether licensed or not, HMO status brings additional problems and expenses for the owner of any property with **five or more** tenants. In this case a bathroom with WC and basin will not be enough. The following *additional* facilities will be required:

- ◆ A WC and wash basin separate from the bathroom.
- ◆ A wash basin in every living unit (i.e. bedrooms and living rooms).
- ◆ Hot and cold taps to all basins.

The cost of altering a property to provide these facilities will be prohibitive for most landlords. The effect of these regulations will be to reduce the maximum number of tenants, in most properties, to four.

Landlords should not necessarily be discouraged by all this from going down the HMO route. Some sensible precautions, however, are certainly called for. Avoid the formula 5 + 3. Five tenants or more plus a three-storey building = mandatory licensing. Where the property does not have wash basins in every bedroom and a separate WC and wash basin (see above), settle for a maximum of four tenants. If licensing is unavoidable, check what fees are being charged in the relevant local authority. Check the council's policy on additional, discretionary licensing. Avoid areas where this is likely.

TENANTS IN PLACE

Buying a property with tenants already in place would seem to be the perfect formula for the property investor. No need to look for tenants. No need to agonise over whether to use agents. No need to pay agents' fees. No need, in fact, to do anything apart from completing the purchase. After that, an instant stream of income!

A golden opportunity or a minefield? Tread very carefully. It is a minefield!

◆ Ask yourself why the property is not being sold with vacant possession. Is it a case of a landlord retiring and liquidating his stock or a landlord desperate to get out? Is it a property that will appeal only to the investor? After all, if the owner waits for his tenants to go he will have two markets to target – the investor and the residential buyer.

- Many of these properties are sold at auction. Always check the auction's legal pack for information about the tenants (see Chapter 17).

- Is there a tenancy agreement in place? If not, when did the tenants move in? If it was prior to 15 January 1989 the tenants are regulated tenants and you should walk away as quickly as possible. The rent can be set as a fair rent by the Residential Property Tribunal Service (always less than the market rent) if the landlord and tenant are in dispute. In addition, such tenants are virtually impossible to remove.

- If the tenants arrived after 15 January 1989 and there is no agreement in place, you should insist on a new shorthold tenancy agreement as a condition of the purchase.

- If there is an assured shorthold tenancy (AST) in place, check that you are happy with all the details, terms and conditions, in particular the persons named on the agreement (are they the same people?) and the term remaining on the tenancy.

- As soon as the AST comes to an end, replace it with your own and start afresh.

- Ask for the original references and make your own checks.

- Carry out credit checks on the tenants.

- Check that gas certificates are up to date and all furniture complies with the Furniture and Furnishings (Fire, Safety) Regulations 1988.

- Provide your own inventory.

- Advise the tenants, in writing, of your name and address.

Under sections 47 and 48 of the Landlord and Tenant Act 1987, the tenant must be provided with the name and address of the landlord. Otherwise he cannot be compelled to pay rent and any action for repossession can be successfully resisted.

After all that you may wonder if buying a property with tenants in place is such a good idea!

The Tenancy Agreement

ASSURED SHORTHOLD TENANCY

The assured shorthold tenancy (AST) revolutionised the rental market in the UK when it was introduced by the Housing Act 1988. For the first time it was possible to terminate a tenancy and gain possession without too much fuss and bother at the end of an agreed fixed term (normally six months) or any time thereafter, provided two months' notice had been given. The tenant no longer had a right to indefinite security of tenure. In addition, the concept of the market rent was accepted as the norm and, in the case of a tenant refusing to leave, a procedure of accelerated possession was introduced, bringing to an end the often interminable delays that had previously plagued the market.

Tenancies created before 15 January 1989 are of an entirely different character. Regulated or Rent Act tenancies, as they are called, can have their rents set or regulated by the Residential Property Tribunal Service, in the event of a dispute, and give the tenant almost total security of tenure.

In addition to the AST, the Housing Act 1988 introduced a tenancy called the assured tenancy. This should not be confused with the assured shorthold tenancy (AST). While both tenancies have features in common, they also have a crucial difference – in the case of an AST it is enough for a court that the fixed term of the tenancy has expired. The landlord will have to be granted possession. In the case of the assured tenancy the expiry of the tenancy agreement is not in itself grounds for automatic repossession. If the tenant refuses to go a court order is needed to evict him. It is for the judge to decide. It is also possible for the tenancy to be passed on to a spouse or partner on death. Needless to say, this strange anomaly does not make the assured tenancy an attractive proposition for landlords. For this reason it fell quickly into disuse. There is even provision now to make sure an assured tenancy is not created accidentally. After 28 February 1997 it will be assumed that a new tenancy is an assured shorthold tenancy or AST unless it is expressly stated that it is to be an assured tenancy.

A standard tenancy agreement for an AST can be purchased on the web from legal stationers such as Oyez or in the high street from WH Smith. They are also available to members of landlord associations. Standard ASTs will contain the basic clauses covering essential details such as the following:

- The address of the property.
- The landlord's details (name and address must be provided, as stipulated by sections 47 and 48 of the Landlord and Tenant Act 1987).
- The rent.
- When and how it should be paid.
- The deposit.
- The term of the tenancy. The tenants are contractually obliged to stay for the full term of the tenancy or pay the rent due for the full term.

It will also cover standard terms and conditions applicable to most tenancies, such as the tenant's duty to pay his or her council tax and other bills and the landlord's undertaking to insure the property against fire and other normal risks.

It is unlikely, however, that a standard AST agreement will cover everything you need and amendments will have to be made. You may have particular concerns about, for example, pets or smoking or weeding the garden.

UNFAIR TERMS

Your additional terms and conditions, however, must be *reasonable* and should not fall foul of the Unfair Terms in Consumer Contracts Regulations 1999. The Office of Fair Trading issues a leaflet for consumers (readily available on the OFT website) covering unfair terms in tenancy agreements. Examples include requiring the tenant to pay for repairs which are the landlord's responsibility or a requirement that the landlord should be able to enter the premises as and when he likes, without giving notice. Such terms would be deemed unfair and unenforceable.

TIP
It is always best to seek legal advice before amending a tenancy agreement.

JOINT OR SINGLE AGREEMENTS

When letting a property to a group of, say, four students, you can draw up a joint agreement they all sign. Alternatively you can provide four separate tenancy agreements. Occasionally you will have no choice in the matter as the students may not all arrive conveniently at the same time. You may have to fill the house, room by room, over a period of time, providing individual contracts as you go along.

Where you do have a choice, however, the joint agreement is far and away the best. The reason is this: a joint agreement means that all are jointly and severally (to use the legal jargon) responsible for the rent. Although the tenants may pay their individual share separately, they are each responsible for the *total* rent. If someone leaves, therefore, or fails to pay his rent, the others are legally bound to make up the shortfall. This certainly concentrates the mind! The real benefit of this arrangement can be seen when someone leaves unexpectedly. It is in everyone's interest to find a replacement as soon as possible. The onus passes from the landlord to the remaining tenants.

Now consider the single tenancy agreement. Here the agreement begins and ends with the tenant:

♦ If he leaves or fails to pay his rent this is a matter of no concern to the other tenants. The landlord has to sort it out.

♦ With separate agreements there is the further disadvantage that the local council will expect the landlord to pay the council tax. The tenants would have to agree to reimburse him the cost.

♦ A further problem can arise at the end of a tenancy. Tenants pay a damage deposit to cover the cost of any damage they may have caused. However, while responsibility for damage to an individual bedroom can safely be assigned to the occupant of that room, what about the common areas, such as the lounge and the bathroom? A tenant could well claim that he was not responsible. In the case of a joint tenancy, *all* are responsible. The cost of the damage is deducted from the total deposit and the remainder apportioned equally between the tenants. Any disputes about individual responsibility will have to be resolved among themselves.

Joint tenancy agreements are always preferable.

STAMP DUTY ON TENANCY AGREEMENT

Fortunately, the question of Stamp Duty (more accurately, Stamp Duty Land Tax or SDLT) is no longer as complicated as it used to be. From December 2003 *no* Stamp Duty is required on a tenancy agreement if the rent in total (i.e. over the whole duration of the tenancy) is £60,000 or less. For tenancies starting after 17 March 2005 this figure has been raised to £120,000. For rents above these figures, a duty of 1% is payable within 30 days. There is no longer a requirement to send the agreement away to the Stamp Office. It is the *tenant* who is liable to pay the SDLT, but the landlord should make this clear, preferably in writing, at the outset. For detailed information on the SDLT, see the Inland Revenue's website (www.inlandrevenue.gov.uk/so) or call 0845 603 0135.

LATEST VERSION OF AGREEMENT

Always use an up-to date version of an AST. This is particularly important in relation to such matters as unfair terms and the requirement that plain English should be used at all times. Courts will show no mercy if the AST you are using is not correctly drafted. There is also a legal requirement to include in the AST a clear statement of how the tenant's deposit is to be protected (see Chapter 25).

PERIODIC TENANCY

When a tenancy agreement comes to an end, it can be replaced by a new agreement. If nothing is done, however, the tenancy becomes a periodic tenancy. The period in question depends on how the rent is paid. If it is paid monthly then the tenancy is a monthly periodic tenancy. Nothing else changes. All the terms and conditions of the original agreement still apply.

To-do List

Apart from the tenancy agreement itself, a number of other important tasks need to be carried out before your tenants move in.

DAMAGE DEPOSIT

Collect the damage deposit. Traditionally, the deposit has always been set as a month's rent. Unfortunately, many tenants take the view that it can serve instead as their last month's rent! When the tenancy is coming to an end, therefore, they simply don't pay the last month's rent, allowing the landlord to keep the deposit instead. While this may make perfect sense to the tenant it leaves the landlord in an impossible position. If no damage has been done and no deductions from the deposit are required, then all is well. If the situation is different, however, the landlord has nothing from the tenant to cover the cost. The only solution is to require a deposit greater than a month's rent (e.g. five or six weeks or one month plus £100). If the tenant behaves as described above, then the landlord still has some deposit left for any contingencies. Only accept a cheque for the deposit if there are at least five working days for the cheque to clear. Otherwise cash. (For details of how the Housing Act 2004 affects the holding of deposits see Chapter 25.)

BANK STANDING ORDER

Collect the first month's rent and arrange a bank standing order for subsequent payments. The rent, like the deposit, should be in cash unless there is ample time for a cheque to clear. Future payments should be accepted by standing order only.

Provide a standing order form *yourself* and have it completed and signed. Then post it *yourself* to the appropriate bank. It is a simple matter to draft a standing order but, if you join one of the landlord associations, you will be able to download one from their website.

INVENTORY

Provide an inventory. This is a list of every item in the property and a statement of the condition it is in (whether brand new, damaged or worn) when the new tenant takes up residence. Leave a space against each entry to allow for any comments the tenant may wish to add. Landlord and tenant should then sign and date the agreed inventory and a copy should be left with the tenant. Ready-to-use inventories can be obtained from any of the landlord associations. They can also be downloaded free from www.landlordzone.co.uk.

A detailed inventory does not guarantee that disputes will not arise at the end of the tenancy. For this reason always photograph or video everything in sight before your tenant moves in. Make sure such photographic evidence is dated.

If you don't wish to deal with the inventory yourself, you might consider having the inventory drawn up independently by an inventory clerk. There are, of course, costs associated with this option. The clerk will charge the landlord when checking in the tenants and will expect the tenants to pay when checking out. Check *Yellow Pages* and the Internet for local inventory clerks and their costs.

At the end of the tenancy, landlord and tenant should meet again at the property to go through the inventory and assess the condition of the items listed.

The importance of an inventory is highlighted by the Tenancy Deposit Scheme introduced by the Housing Act 2004 (see Chapter 25). If there is a dispute about the return of the tenant's deposit (or part of the deposit), this must now be resolved by an independent arbitration service. Questions about any damage you claim the tenant has inflicted on your property will centre entirely on the contents of the inventory. If there is no inventory at all, your case is lost. It is also worth bearing in mind there will usually be an inventory clerk on the panel of arbitrators.

UTILITY COMPANIES AND LOCAL COUNCIL

Contact utility companies and the local council and advise them of the date your tenants moved in (failure to do this could result in utility and council tax bills being sent to *you*). Provide the tenants with contact details for the utility companies and council tax department of the local council, and provide the utility companies and local council with contact details for your tenants. Leave nothing to chance!

Part Five

Legal Matters

The law makes itself felt at every turn in the world of landlord and tenant. From the Law of Property Act 1925 to the Housing Act 2004 it seems our legislators cannot resist the temptation to intervene with more and more legal requirements and constraints. While it is impossible (and unnecessary) to have a working knowledge of every aspect of landlord and tenant legislation, there are certain areas that do require particular attention. These are likely to be encountered on a regular, if not routine, basis by the long-term landlord.

(25)

Tenants' Deposits

Damage deposits, paid by tenants at the beginning of a tenancy, have always been a bone of contention, with tenants frequently complaining that some or all of their deposit has been unfairly retained by the landlord.

The Housing Act 2004 sought to sweep all this aside and put in place a system that would be totally transparent, protect the deposit from the beginning to end of the tenancy and provide a fair system of arbitration when all else fails. The deposit schemes took effect from 6 April 2007 and apply to all assured shorthold tenancies (ASTs). Other tenancy agreements are not affected.

TENANCY DEPOSIT SCHEMES (TDSs)

The most important change, introduced, by the Act, is the requirement for the landlord to use one of two tenancy deposit schemes (TDSs) when taking a deposit from a tenant. If the deposit is not covered by a TDS, the landlord is not allowed to take one at all. In addition, if he fails to comply with the rules of the chosen TDS, the landlord will not be able to recover possession of the property in the normal way (i.e. by serving a section 21 notice) until all the scheme requirements have been fulfilled. The landlord has 14 days from the date he receives the deposit (*not* from the start date of the tenancy which could be some time later) to comply with his obligations and to inform the tenant in writing of the details of the scheme (the prescribed information).

Scope of TDS

The following points should be noted:

♦ Only ASTs require a deposit protection scheme. A tenancy with a rent of more than £25,000 a year is not an AST and would therefore not be affected. Likewise, neither a company let nor a holiday let would come within the scope of the Act, and the deposit for these would not need to be protected.

♦ AST agreements entered into *before* the deposit scheme was introduced are not affected while they remain in place, so long as they continue as periodic tenancies (i.e. without a new agreement being drawn up at the end of the tenancy term). If, however, a new tenancy agreement *is* drawn up, then the original deposit will need to be protected at the same time.

Types of TDS

The landlord has a choice of two types of scheme.

Custodial

In this case the landlord collects the deposit in the normal way but must then pass it on, in full, within 14 days, to the scheme administrator. It is held within the scheme, gathering interest over the term of the tenancy, until it is paid out to the tenant, with interest, at the end of the tenancy. The scheme cannot contain any cash from any other source and the interest rate is set by the government.

Insurance based

In this case the landlord keeps the deposit in the normal way and undertakes to reimburse the insurance-based scheme if it is has to pay the deposit to the tenant before receiving it from the landlord.

Normally it is only in the event of a dispute that the landlord will be obliged to transfer the deposit (or the disputed part of a deposit) to the chosen deposit scheme. The scheme then holds it until the dispute is resolved. If the landlord fails to transfer the deposit to the scheme, the scheme administrator will pay the tenant and then claim the money back from the landlord. If the landlord fails to comply with his obligation in this regard, the scheme will claim the money back from the insurance company underwriting the scheme.

In the absence of any dispute, the landlord will be expected to return the deposit to the tenant within 10 days of the tenant asking for it. If the landlord fails to comply with this request, the tenant can complain to the scheme administrator, who will direct the landlord to pay the outstanding amount into the scheme within 10 days of being directed to do so. Again, should the landlord fail to comply, the scheme administrator will make a claim against the insurance company underwriting the scheme.

The tenancy agreement

An AST agreement *must* now contain a clause to indicate that the deposit will be protected under the TDS.

Joint tenancies

Where there is more than one person on a tenancy agreement, the situation regarding deposit protection is more complicated. Usually each tenant will have made an individual contribution to the deposit. How is that protected? It is not uncommon for a tenant to leave and be replaced in the course of the tenancy. What happens to his deposit? Does the scheme administrator communicate with each tenant individually?

The total deposit, in the case of a joint tenancy, is seen by the scheme administrator as a single deposit, regardless of each tenant's contribution to it. For ease of administration, the landlord or agent must ask the tenants to nominate a lead tenant who will be the point of contact for the scheme administrators (although the names of *all* the tenants will appear on the paperwork). If the lead tenant, or any other, leaves before the end of the tenancy, the scheme must be notified so that new paperwork can be issued. The custodial scheme will not release part of the deposit if a tenant leaves. The outgoing and incoming tenants will have to come to their own arrangement. This could involve the new tenant paying his portion of the deposit to the outgoing tenant. Where a departing tenant is not replaced at all there is no solution to the problem! In the case of the insurance-based schemes, the landlord still holds the deposit and there is scope for more flexibility.

Tenant's address

A peculiarity of the schemes is the requirement to have a correspondence address, other than that of the property to be rented, for the tenant or the lead tenant. The reason is that, in the event of a dispute at the end of a tenancy, the tenant will no longer be in the rented property. Also, at the beginning of the tenancy, the deposit may have been paid some time before the tenant takes occupation. In both cases the scheme administrator needs an address for correspondence.

Third-party deposits

It doesn't matter who actually pays the deposit (it could be a relative, for example, or a local authority), it must be protected if the tenancy is an AST.

Paperwork

When a deposit is registered and an application for protection received, the insurance-based scheme Tenancy Deposit Solutions Ltd issues a deposit protection certificate to the landlord. It will contain the following details:

◆ Name, address and telephone number of the landlord.
◆ Details of letting agent (if applicable).
◆ Property address to be rented.
◆ Name of lead tenant and alternative address (see above).
◆ Names of other tenants.
◆ Name and address of any interested party (if applicable).
◆ Start date of tenancy.
◆ Date deposit paid.
◆ Amount of deposit.
◆ Period of protection. This will be from the start date until the deposit is unprotected. An additional 90 days will be allowed, during which a complaint can be made, if the deposit has been unprotected by the landlord alone.
◆ Address and contact details of the alternative dispute resolution service for the scheme (see below).

The certificate will already have been signed by the scheme administrator. Both landlord and tenant will now be required to sign in order to confirm the accuracy of the information contained in it.

Along with the deposit protection certificate, the scheme (looking ahead to the end of the tenancy) also provides, for landlord and tenant, a 'request to unprotect deposit' form. If there is no dispute about the deposit, both landlord and tenant sign the appropriate section of the form and send it to the scheme administrator within 10 days of the end of the tenancy. If there is a dispute, however, the tenant will complete the 'Notification of a deposit complaint' section of the form and return it to the scheme administrator. This must be no earlier than 10 days after the tenancy ends.

Alternative dispute resolution (ADR)

All the schemes have a system of arbitration for resolving disputes when landlord and tenant cannot agree. The purpose here is to avoid costly and time-consuming legal action. However, if either landlord or tenant objects to the ADR process the dispute can still be taken to court. If the ADR is used, however, both parties must agree to abide by the outcome and cannot subsequently take court action.

An application to have the dispute settled by the ADR service must be made within 28 days of the end of the tenancy. If one of the parties cannot be located or refuses to co-operate, a single claim can be made.

With regards to the deposit itself, there are some differences between the custodial and the insurance-based schemes where a dispute is involved:

◆ In the case of the custodial scheme the deposit is already in the hands of the scheme administrators. Where an insurance-based scheme has been used, the landlord holds the deposit but must now hand it over (or the disputed part of it) to the scheme *before* the arbitration process begins.

◆ In the case of the custodial scheme the entire deposit will be retained until the matter is resolved, even though only part of it may be in dispute. In the case of the insurance-based schemes, only the disputed part is retained by the scheme as only this portion has been handed over. For example, where there is a deposit in place of £700 and the landlord claims he needs £200 to effect repairs to his property, he will return £500 to the tenant and, if the tenant disputes his claim, transfer the £200 to the scheme for arbitration.

There are no costs involved for landlord or tenant in using the ADR service.

Scheme providers

The Deposit Protection Service (the custodial scheme) is run by Computershare Investor Services PLC, a company that runs a similar scheme in Australia.

There are two insurance-based schemes to choose from: Tenancy Deposit Solutions Ltd (in association with the National Landlords' Association) and The Dispute Service Ltd. The first is aimed mainly at landlords while The Dispute Service is largely used by letting agents with a large number of deposits to protect.

Costs

There are no costs for either party in using the custodial scheme. The insurance-based schemes, however, are funded by insurance premiums and these, along with other administrative costs, are paid by the landlord. The fees come in the form of a single joining fee, followed by a separate fee for each deposit protected. There is a slight reduction in costs for members of landlords' associations. There are no cost implications for the tenant, and neither landlord nor agent can pass on *their* costs to the tenant.

Penalties

Failure to comply with the rules for deposit schemes can have severe consequences for the landlord:

◆ Failure to carry out the initial requirements of the scheme within 14 days and failure to provide the tenant with the appropriate information about the scheme within 14 days will mean that the landlord cannot use the section 21 notice procedure (under the Housing Act 1988) to recover possession of the property. This would mean, in effect, that the landlord would need a court order to evict the tenant – something the court would not grant.

◆ A tenant can apply to the court to have his deposit returned if the landlord has not complied with the rules of the scheme. If, by the time the case comes to court, the landlord has still not returned the deposit, the court *must* order him to pay three times the value of the deposit to the tenant, within 10 days.

TDSs: SUMMARY

Do you need to take a deposit at all? There is no legal requirement to do so. In practice, with your type of tenant, have you ever needed to retain part or all of a deposit at the end of a tenancy? Or have you found that the deposit is largely irrelevant, in any case, because many of your tenants simply don't pay the last month's rent? If you have difficulty letting your property, would you have an edge over other landlords by making a point of *not* requiring a deposit? If you routinely take a guarantee from a third party (e.g. for student letting), do you feel this is protection enough?

It is possible to insure (at a price) against damage caused by tenants (see 'Useful addresses' for companies offering this service). This avoids having to take a deposit. The drawback is that your prospective tenants will be fully checked out (credit checks included) by the insuring company and will be rejected unless squeaky clean. If they are good enough to be accepted, you might well ask if you need to bother with a deposit anyway, or go to the expense of an insurance scheme.

If your tenant has a tenancy agreement that predates 6 April 2007 (when the new scheme came into force), think carefully before you draw up a new agreement when the term of that tenancy expires. Allowing the tenancy to continue as a periodic tenancy instead avoids the need to protect the original deposit.

When deciding between the custodial and insurance-based schemes, consider the financial implications. The custodial scheme costs nothing but will deprive you of the deposit. If, in practice, your deposits help with your cash-flow, this may influence your decision. If you normally put the cash in a deposit account you will lose the interest. Is the cost of the scheme, over the average term of your tenancies, more or less than the interest you would earn over the same term?

If you use a letting agent check that they are complying with the law and using an appropriate deposit scheme. Get confirmation of this *in writing*.

As there is now an independent arbitration system to resolve disputes, it is vital that you are well prepared to defend your position. To that end a comprehensive and detailed inventory is essential (there may well be an inventory clerk on the panel of arbitrators). While an inventory is not a requirement, you are guaranteed to fail if you don't have one. If you have not bothered with inventories up to now, it is time to start.

By far the best safeguard, in addition to the written inventory, is to take timed and dated photographs or video footage of everything in sight. Many disputes centre round wear and tear (not covered by damage deposits) versus serious damage (which certainly is). A photograph speaks volumes.

If you find yourself in dispute over the deposit, obtain estimates (two or three) for any repair work you claim needs to be carried out. These should be presented, along with the inventory, photos, etc., to the arbitration panel. Make it as easy as possible for the panel to reach a quick decision in your favour.

Make sure your tax affairs are in order! It would be foolhardy to believe that the taxman will not gain access to the wealth of information so readily available now in TDSs. The scheme rules and regulations of Tenancy Deposit Solutions Ltd state clearly that data may be handed over to 'regulators, industry bodies and other organizations for the purpose of fraud prevention and money-laundering prevention, or if there are concerns over your activities'. You have been warned!

26

Recovering Possession

There will come a time when you will want to have your property back. Usually this will be when a tenancy has come to an end. Occasionally, it will be because the tenants are seriously misbehaving – most commonly by not paying the rent. This may be well before the end of the tenancy. The point to remember in both cases is that you cannot simply take possession of your property because you feel you have a right to do so. Evicting a tenant, for whatever reason, has been a criminal offence since the Protection from Eviction Act 1977.

A legal notice has to be served, regardless of the circumstances. There is also a system for accelerated possession which can be used under certain circumstances.

SECTION 21 NOTICE

For many landlords, a section 21 notice is the only one they will encounter on a regular basis. This is the notice, as stipulated by the Housing Act 1988, which needs to be served by the landlord if he requires possession at the end of the fixed term of the tenancy. The notice needs to state simply that:

- the landlord requires possession
- that this cannot happen before the end of the tenancy
- and not until two months have elapsed after the notice is served

◆ and, in the case of a *periodic tenancy*, not until two months after the last date of a period of the tenancy.

The following points should be noted:

◆ The notice must be *in writing*. The Housing Act 1996, amending the Housing Act 1988, introduced this requirement.

◆ There is no particular form required for this notice. Do not, however, do it yourself! Obtain a ready-made form from one of the landlord associations.

◆ The notice can be served at any time but it is good practice to serve it at the start of the tenancy. This neatly avoids any difficulties that might be encountered in serving it later!

◆ If a new tenancy agreement replaces the first, a new notice will have to be served.

◆ The expiry date of the notice should be *after* the last day of the tenancy. If it is the last day or before it will be invalid. The last day of a tenancy is the day before the rent is due. The term of the notice should be at least two calendar months. Take the following example: a tenancy has a term of six months from 1 March 2007 to 31 August 2007. If notice is served on 15 May, possession can be required after 31 August 2007. If notice is not served until, say, 15 July 2007, the earliest expiry date will be after 15 September 2007.

◆ If the tenancy has become a periodic tenancy (i.e. the fixed term has expired and no new tenancy agreement has been put in place) the term should be two calendar months after the last date of a period (i.e. the day before the rent is due again). If, for example, the notice is issued in the middle of the period (i.e. before the last date of that period), then the term of the notice will need to be more than two months (i.e. what is left of that period plus two months). Take the following example: a tenancy agreement runs from 1 March 2007 to 31 August 2007. It then becomes a periodic tenancy. If notice is served on 15 September, possession can be required after 30 November 2007.

◆ The notice can be served by hand or posted. If posted, always use recorded delivery. Another sensible precaution is to use the next-day delivery service provided by the post office and to keep the receipt. In this way you know exactly when the notice will arrive.

◆ If a tenant fails to comply with a section 21 notice, the landlord will need to take action through the county court for the area in which the property is situated. The county court form required here is N5B.

SECTION 8 NOTICE

This is the unpleasant, but sometimes, necessary business of removing a tenant who is in breach of his agreement and simply refuses to leave. A section 8 notice (under the Housing Act 1988) covers a number of grounds on which possession can be sought (17 in all), including damage to the property, damage to the furniture or causing a nuisance to neighbours. It also covers circumstances where the landlord wishes to return to what was his principal home, an educational institute wishes to recover a room in their halls of residence or a religious body wishes to remove one of their ministers. But the most significant grounds for possession, for most landlords, relate to the non-payment of rent.

The following points about the section 8 notice should be noted:

- Unlike the section 21, there is a prescribed form for the section 8. Only this form can be used. Obtain a copy from legal stationers or a landlords' association.

- The form requires the following details: all tenants' names, the address of the property, the grounds for serving the notice requiring possession, an explanation as to why these grounds are relied upon, the earliest date that court proceedings can begin, the landlord's name, address and phone numbers.

- The grounds for issuing the notice must be clearly stated.

- The notice lasts a year. In other words, a summons for possession can be issued during this period, but not after.

- The original tenancy agreement must have contained the landlord's name and address (rent cannot be demanded without this).

- If there is more than one landlord on the tenancy agreement, one can sign on behalf of the other.

- If there is more than one tenant on the agreement, however, *each tenant* needs to be served with a notice.

- The earliest date for court proceedings needs to be specified in the notice, but this will not be the same for all grounds that can be used for requiring possession. For example, if the ground for possession is that alternative accommodation has been offered to the tenant (ground 9), the earliest date for court proceedings will be two months after the notice is served. In the case of rent arrears, however (ground 8), it is two weeks.

It is essential to follow the instructions on the form with great care. If the notice is not correctly completed it can be rejected on this basis alone.

As already indicated, the reason most commonly stated for possession is non-payment of rent. This is covered by grounds 8, 10 and 11 and particular attention should be paid to these.

Ground 8

This is the most important ground as far as the landlord is concerned because it is mandatory. If the case is proved, then the court *must* grant possession.

The following are the essential features of ground 8:

♦ Rent must be in arrears by at least eight weeks (for a weekly tenancy) or two months (for a monthly tenancy) at the time the notice is served.

♦ The rent must also be in arrears, to this extent at least, at the time the case is heard.

♦ The onus of proof rests entirely on the landlord who will have to have all the necessary documentation to prove his case.

You can see at a glance both the strength of ground 8 and its weakness. If both rent-arrears requirements are met, then possession is guaranteed. If, on the other hand, the tenant pays something before the hearing, reducing the rent outstanding at the time of the hearing to below the above levels, then ground 8 will fail. For this reason other grounds should, if possible, also be cited. These are grounds 10 and 11.

Grounds 10 and 11

Unlike ground 8, these grounds are not mandatory. They are discretionary. It is for the court to decide whether or not to grant possession on these grounds.

Ground 10 allows for rent arrears that are less than the levels required for ground 8. Ground 11 covers regular and persistent delays in making rent payments. As with ground 8, the onus of proof lies with the landlord.

If a tenant fails to comply with a section 8 notice, the landlord will need to take action through the county court for the area in which the property is situated. The county court forms required are N119 and N5.

ACCELERATED POSSESSION

In certain circumstances the whole process of recovering possession can be considerably speeded up by using the accelerated possession procedure, which is allowed in certain limited circumstances. The essential features of the system are as follows:

◆ It is applicable only where the tenancy agreement used was an Assured Shorthold Tenancy.

◆ The fixed term of the tenancy must have expired and the required two months' notice must have been served.

◆ The original section 21 notice must not have required possession before the end of any current fixed-term tenancy.

- In the case of a periodic tenancy, the date possession is required must be the last day of a tenancy period.

- It can be used for recovering possession only, not rent arrears.

- An order for possession cannot take effect until after six months from the start of the tenancy. In other words, if a tenancy agreement was entered into for less than six months it will still not be possible to get an order for possession until after six months.

- There is no need for a court hearing. Written submissions alone are accepted.

- It cannot be used for seeking possession on grounds of rent arrears (grounds 8, 10, 11) for which a court hearing is required.

The county court form required in this case is N5B, and help on completing it can be obtained on Her Majesty's Court Service website (www.hmcourts-service.gov.uk).

27

Landlord's Obligations

The cost of maintaining a property can come as a shock to a first-time landlord. It seems that something always needs to be done and, in most cases, done urgently. Whether it is a case of the boiler breaking down or the roof leaking, tenants naturally expect something to be done about it. But in some areas it is not the tenant but the law that insists on action, with dire consequences for failure to comply. These legal areas of responsibility need to be known and understood fully.

REPAIRS

The Landlord and Tenant Act 1985, section 11, sets out clearly the landlord's obligations, in law, regarding the state of repair of the rented property. It states that the landlord undertakes (whether he knows this or not!):

(a) to keep in repair the structure and exterior of the dwelling-house (including drains, gutters and external pipes);

(b) to keep in repair and proper working order the installations in the dwelling-house for the supply of water, gas and electricity and for sanitation (including basins, sinks, baths and sanitary conveniences, but not other fixtures, fittings and appliances for making use of the supply of water, gas or electricity);

(c) to keep in repair and proper working order the

installations in the dwelling-house for space heating and water heating.

It can be seen from this that there is very little the landlord is not legally responsible for. Blocked drains and leaking downpipes outside the building may not bother the tenant, but it is the landlord's duty to keep them in good repair. Inside the property, while it is the tenant who usually *pays* for gas, electricity and water supplies, it is the landlord who has to make sure they can *receive and use* them. For that reason the landlord is legally obliged to keep water pipes, gas pipes, electricity cables, sinks, baths, etc., in good order. As heating and hot water are vital requirements in any household, they get specific mention in the Act. There is a legal obligation to fix that boiler!

It isn't, however, all bad news. The Act states that the landlord is *not* expected:

(a) to carry out works or repairs for which the lessee is liable by virtue of his duty to use the premises in a tenant-like manner, or would be so liable but for an express covenant on his part;

(b) to rebuild or reinstate the premises in the case of destruction or damage by fire, or by tempest, flood or other inevitable accident, or

(c) to keep in repair or maintain anything which the lessee is entitled to remove from the dwelling-house.

In other words, if the tenant trashes the place, he cannot expect the landlord to put it right! If the building is destroyed in a freak storm, the tenant cannot insist that it be rebuilt just for him, and if the tenant's own television has stopped working, he cannot insist that the landlord repair it.

FURNITURE AND FURNISHINGS

A fire in the home is a risk everybody has to face. When it comes to rented property, however, it isn't only the occupant who should take precautions. The landlord has legal obligations in one specific area of fire risk – furniture and furnishings.

If the property is furnished, the furniture and furnishings provided must comply with the Furniture and Furnishings (Fire) (Safety) Regulations 1988 (as amended in 1989 and 1993), and the landlord is obliged to ascertain that they do. These regulations set down standards manufacturers must meet in respect of levels of fire resistance in any upholstered product used in the home (curtains and carpets are not covered by the regulations), whether new or second hand.

For most landlords, whether involved in residential or holiday lets, this is straightforward enough. They must comply with the regulations and only provide compliant furniture and furnishings. In some cases, however, the letting may not be deemed to be a business activity. In other words, the landlord does not see the property primarily as a source of income. This would be the case, for example, if he lets his own home for a short time while travelling abroad. The test is whether the landlord is using the property as a *business*. If he is he must comply.

If an agent is used to manage the property, the question arises as to whether it is the agent or the landlord who is the supplier of the furniture and therefore subject to the regulations. The answer lies in the contract. If the tenancy agreement is between the tenant and landlord, then the landlord is the supplier. This would clearly be the situation in the majority of cases.

Labels

All new furniture must have a label attached showing that the item complies with the regulations. With the exception of mattresses and bed-bases, the label must be permanent (i.e. not easily removed without damaging the furniture). It is this label that the landlord must look out for. No item of upholstered furniture should be provided without one. Items on which labels are required include the following:

◆ *Bedroom:* pillows, beds, mattresses, padded headboards.
◆ *Lounge:* armchairs, covers for armchairs, futons, sofa-beds, chairs, bean bags, cushions.
◆ *Kitchen:* padded seats for chairs.

The trading standards department of the local authority enforces the regulations, and they should be consulted if a landlord is in any doubt about how the regulations affect him.

GAS SAFETY

Like furniture, gas poses an obvious risk if things go wrong. Apart from the danger of explosion and fire, there is the possibility of carbon monoxide poisoning through faulty or incorrectly installed appliances. The Gas Safety (Installation and Use) Regulations 1998 set out strict rules regarding the supply and installation of gas appliances and place responsibility on the landlord to ensure that all gas equipment provided by him is safe.

Among the many requirements of the Act are the following:

- Only a CORGI (Council for Registered Gas Installers) registered engineer can install or carry out maintenance work on gas appliances.

- The engineer must carry out a specific list of tests and checks after completing his work.

- Appliances in bathrooms and bedrooms must be *room* sealed. 'Sealed' in this case means sealed from the room, with air being drawn in from outside and waste gases vented to the outside.

- Gas appliances known or thought to be unsafe must not be used.

- In the event of a gas leak or build-up of carbon monoxide, the occupier (i.e. the tenant) has a legal duty to inform the supplier and do what he can to cut off the supply. If the property is empty, this responsibility lies with the landlord or agent.

- If any alterations are made to the property, checks must be made to see if existing gas installations are adversely affected by the work.

The landlord
For the landlord specifically, there is a list of legal obligations in relation to gas supply. He must:

- ensure that all gas equipment (appliances, pipes, flues) is properly maintained at all times;

- arrange an annual check of appliances and flues by a CORGI-registered engineer;

◆ in the case of a *new* tenancy, ensure that all gas appliances and flues have been checked in the 12 months before the tenancy began;

◆ keep records of safety checks for two years;

◆ provide *all* tenants with a copy of the annual check within 28 days of it being carried out; and

◆ provide new tenants with a copy before they move in.

A landlord cannot avoid his legal responsibility in this matter by delegating the task of annual safety checks to his tenants, even if they agree to undertake this task.

Agents
When an agent is used to manage a property, the landlord should ensure that the contract between himself and the agent states clearly who is to arrange the annual safety checks and who is to keep the records.

Penalties
Falling foul of the Act is a serious matter and a breach constitutes a criminal offence. The consequences can range from a heavy fine to imprisonment.

ELECTRICAL SAFETY
All electrical appliances provided by the landlord (Electrical Equipment [Safety] Regulations 1994) must be safe to use – microwaves, toasters, cookers, vacuum cleaners, fridges, freezers, tumble dryers, etc. This includes sockets, plugs and leads required

to supply power for the appliances. This applies whether the appliances are new or second hand (appliances provided by the tenant are *not* the landlord's responsibility). When deciding what electrical appliances to supply, it is worth asking which are essential and which, perhaps, are not. That sandwich maker or toaster you are thinking of buying could misbehave and land you in trouble! It is also worthwhile keeping guarantees and receipts for any new appliances you buy. You never know when you might need them! With second-hand equipment the situation is more problematic. Either don't buy at all or have them checked immediately (see below). The cost involved (for a second-hand toaster!) could well make this option unviable.

It is worth bearing in mind that failure to comply with the regulations is a criminal offence and can carry any of the following penalties:

♦ A prison term of up to six months and a fine of £5,000 for each faulty appliance.

♦ In the event of death, a prosecution for manslaughter is possible.

♦ The tenant can also sue you!

Regular checks
Surprisingly, there is no specific legal requirement for regular or annual checks and no requirement for an electrical safety certificate. The contrast with gas safety regulations is marked. Having said that, there are a few reasons at least why you may be well advised to have regular checks carried out:

- The defence of due diligence is accepted by the 1994 Act. This means that, if you can demonstrate that you have done everything possible (that all reasonable measures have been taken) to prevent a problem arising, this will be accepted as a defence. What better way to prove this, then, by having regular checks made, complete with safety certificates?

- If you let property to university students you may find you have no choice in the matter. It is quite common for accommodation departments of universities to insist on an electrical safety certificate every two years.

- It is an accepted fact that insurance companies will do their utmost to avoid meeting a claim. They will be delighted to discover that your electrical appliances are unsafe!

New rules

From January 2005 new regulations, called Part P Building Regulations Electrical Safety, came into force. This stipulates that a lot of electrical work must be carried out by a properly qualified person registered under the 'authorised competent person self-certification scheme'. Apart from relatively minor repair and maintenance work (in areas *other than* kitchens, bathrooms or outdoors), most work needs to be carried out by such a person. Alternatively, the building control department of the local council needs to be informed *before* any work is done. You can imagine where that would lead, both in terms of time and cost!

Areas where electrical work of *any kind* comes under the regulations include kitchens, kitchen diners, bathrooms, shower rooms, bedrooms with shower or basin, gardens, swimming pools, saunas, overhead or under-floor heating, communal parts of purpose-built or converted flats. In other areas, modification to existing electrical installations will be exempt, but *new* installations will not. These areas include stairways, dining rooms, living rooms, halls, studies, integral garages, landings, television rooms and bedrooms.

There is clearly little point in trying to circumvent such tightly drawn regulations. The simplest approach is to use the self-certification schemes and let their members deal with the regulations. The company should be authorised by the National Inspection Council for Electrical Installation Contracting (NICEIC). Among the advantages are the following:

- An electrical installation certificate to prove that the work has been done correctly – invaluable evidence of due diligence (see above).

- No need to deal with the building control department of the council or pay their fees (minimum £50 per job).

- A set complaints procedure if things go wrong.

Part Six

Tax

As the old saying goes: 'the only certainties in life are death and taxes'. While it is not possible to cheat the grim reaper, some may be tempted, when it comes to property investment, to play fast and loose with the taxman. Not a good idea. Consider the following:

◆ The Inland Revenue routinely requires letting agents to hand over details of the landlords on their books. Agents are legally obliged to comply. They are not required, however, to tell their landlords that they are doing so. Indeed, the Revenue advises them that they do *not* have to tell their landlords! If you use an agent and have not declared your rental income, the Revenue will knock on your door sooner or later.

◆ If you let and manage you own property you will, inevitably, advertise for tenants. Whatever you use – newspapers or the web – the Revenue will find you. The days are long gone when the task of trawling through newspaper adverts was a tedious and inefficient chore for junior members of staff. Today it is all done, with frightening efficiency, by highly sophisticated computer software.

◆ If you take a deposit from your tenants (and who doesn't?), you are legally obliged to register and protect it with one of the government-sponsored tenancy deposit schemes (see Chapter 25). These schemes are, by far, the richest and most

comprehensive source of information for the tax-hungry
Revenue.

◆ Lastly, consider the penalties. These can range from charging
interest on what you owe to doubling what you owe!

The taxman, therefore, will have his share. It is essential, however,
to ensure that he does not have more than his share, and there
are many ways of dulling the impact of the tax blow when it
finally comes. The following chapters will consider these in some
detail.

28

Capital Gains Tax

INTRODUCTION

A Capital Gains Tax (CGT) liability can arise when a 'gain' or profit is made on the sale or disposal of an asset. The profit, therefore, on the sale of a property is potentially taxable in this way.

There is, however, no CGT to pay on the sale of *one's own home*. This benefits from **Principal Private Residence** exemption (PPR). However, a profit from the sale of a property that is **not one's principal home** could be subject to CGT. In other words, the difference between the buying and selling price of an investment property is potentially taxable.

While this sounds simple enough, working out the taxable gain itself and the resulting tax liability, **prior to 6 April 2008**, was anything but simple:

+ A distinction was drawn between business and non-business gains. Where the landlord was concerned, letting a holiday home was treated as a business but other forms of residential letting were not! For tax purposes, therefore, most landlords held non-business assets.

+ The difference in the CGT liability between business and non-business gains was considerable. Taper relief (reducing the size of the gain over a period of time) applied to both, but it was far less generous for non-business assets. While the gain on a business asset could be reduced by as much as 75% after just two years, the non-business gain benefited by only a miserly 5% pa reduction, beginning after the first two years. It took ten years to achieve the maximum reduction possible of 40%.

♦ To add further to this confusion there was the issue of *indexation relief* which predated taper relief and which was replaced by it in April 1998. A gain from a property bought before this date and sold after it could be subject to both indexation and taper relief!

♦ When indexation and taper relief were duly accounted for the annual CGT allowance (£9,200 for 07/08) could then be deducted.

♦ Finally, having established the amount of the gain to be taxed it was then necessary to calculate the amount of tax that would actually be payable on it. This wasn't straightforward as it depended on the *other income* of the taxpayer in that tax year. The capital gain was effectively treated as extra income and added to the vendor's other income. This 'top slice' was then taxed at his marginal rate. For a basic rate tax payer the CGT rate was 20%, while for a higher rate tax payer it was 40%. Part of the gain could be taxed at 20% (until the higher rate band was reached) and the rest at 40%.

Confused? The good news is we no longer need to be!

6 APRIL 2008

From this date everything changes and the whole complex system of CGT, as outlined above, is swept aside. The annual CGT allowance remains, but little else is recognisable:

- There is no longer a distinction between business and non-business gains.
- Indexation and taper relief disappear.
- The time the asset is held for is no longer relevant.
- A single flat rate of 18% CGT applies to all gains.

But for the property investor the good news does not stop there. The new system, in the great majority of cases, will result in *far lower capital gains tax bills*. Take the example of a property bought for £150,000 and sold four years later for £200,000. The following are the calculations before and after 6 April 2008:

Pre 6 April 2008

Gain	£50,000
Taper relief	£5,000 (10%)
Adjusted gain	£45,000
CGT allowance	£9,200 (at 07/08 rate)
Taxable gain	£35,800
Tax at 40%	**£14,320**

Post 6 April 2008

Gain	£50,000
CGT allowance	£9,200
Taxable gain	£40,800
Tax at 18%	**£7,344**

CGT AND THE PROPERTY INVESTOR

Everyone has a CGT allowance (adjusted every tax year) which is not subject to tax and which can be used (see the above example) to reduce a taxable gain. Likewise any capital losses incurred can be offset against any gain. For the *property investor*, however, the

Revenue offers further attractive concessions which should be carefully considered when submitting a CGT return.

Purchase costs of property

Expenses incurred 'wholly and exclusively' in the original purchase of the property are allowable. These could be *solicitor's fees, valuation fees, Stamp Duty Land Tax.*

Selling costs

Legal and estate agent costs are allowable.

Capital Improvements

If you have improved the property since you bought it the cost involved is allowable. An extension, a loft conversion or a new kitchen will fall into this category. Keep all the bills. Normal maintenance and repair costs, however, do not count.

Prior occupation

If you occupied the property as your *principal residence* before letting it you can claim CGT exemption for the time it was occupied (*Principal Private Residence* exemption). In addition, in this case, the *last three years* before the property is sold will also be exempt from CGT.

Take the example of a property owned for 10 years and occupied as a main residence for the first three, then let out. No CGT is payable on the first three years and none on the last three. Only four years of the ten are taxable. If, say, the overall gain for the ten years is £60,000 (ie £6,000 a year) then the taxable gain is £24,000 (£6,000 × 4), not £60,000.

This particular scenario, however, has another, highly beneficial twist. There is *further* tax relief, called *Private Letting Relief,* to be claimed in this case.

Private letting relief

This is calculated as the *lesser* of the following:

- The amount exempted due to the years in residence + the last three years, ie £36,000 (£6,000 × 6), in the above case.

- The amount chargeable because of the letting, ie £24,000 (£6,000 × 4).

- £40,000 (for joint ownership the figure is £80,000).

In the above example, therefore, the additional private letting relief is £24,000 and there is no tax at all to pay!

29

CGT Manoeuvres

Apart from making use of all available allowances and reliefs a little careful planning can make further deep inroads into your Capital Gains Tax liability.

DON'T SELL!

Perhaps the most obvious question to ask is whether you need to sell at all to achieve your objective. If the plan is to buy another property, consider whether there is sufficient equity and sufficient rental income in the present property to qualify for a further advance or *drawdown* from the existing lender. This could be used as the deposit for the next purchase, with the balance to come from a further buy-to-let mortgage. The tax advantages are considerable:

1. No CGT to pay at all.
2. Full tax relief on the interest paid on the drawdown funds.
3. Full tax relief on the interest on the new mortgage.
4. You have two properties instead of one, with the prospect of capital growth on both.

In tax terms you are *taking* from the taxman instead of giving to him!

DELAY THE SALE

If you must sell, timing is of the essence. If you are approaching a new tax year consider delaying the sale until 6 April to push the

CGT liability into the next tax year. CGT is paid in full on *31 January following the end of the tax year*. Selling after 6 April delays payment for a further 12 months.

JOINT OWNERSHIP

Before buying a property, bear in mind that CGT will have to be paid at some time in the future. As each person has a CGT allowance (for tax year 07/08 this is £9,200) two people buying a property together will have *two lots of CGT* allowance (£18,400 for 07/08) to claim at the point of sale.

Attempting to deal with this later by converting sole ownership to joint ownership can pose problems. There will be no CGT to pay on transferring a share of the property if the two people concerned are married or in a civil partnership. Otherwise, however, there *will* be a CGT liability. Also, as a transfer of title is involved Stamp Duty Land Tax (SDLT) may be payable. This will depend on whether there is a mortgage on the property. If there is the tax may be payable. As for the mortgage itself, the lender will have to be consulted. He is entitled to object. Careful calculation and professional legal advice are essential before embarking on this course of action. Far better to take this into account at the outset, before any purchase is made.

MOVE IN IMMEDIATELY

The most important tax allowance for any property owner is Principal Private Residence relief or PPR (sometimes called Private Residence Relief or PRR). There is simply no tax to be paid on the sale of your main residence.

It is possible, however, to change your principal residence, to advise the Revenue that you are now living somewhere else and that you wish this new property to be regarded as your main home. If you move into a newly bought property in this way there are several CGT advantages:

1. For the next three years no CGT to pay on the property you have just left, if you decide to sell it.

2. Private Letting Relief if you let your previous home (see Chapter 28).

3. There is no CGT on the property you move into, while you are there, and three years freedom from CGT after you move out. If, therefore, you move into the property, stay there for three years, then move out, let it for three years after that and then sell it, there would be no CGT at all to pay – after six years of ownership. The first three years are exempt because it was your principal residence and the last three years of ownership are exempt because you once lived there!

There are, however, a few points to bear in mind when considering this strategy:

♦ The taxman is no fool. Not only must he be advised of the change of residence, he will expect to see proof of it in the form of council tax bills, utility bills, electoral roll registration etc. The move has to be genuine.

♦ If you want to build a large portfolio of investment properties over a short period of time this is not really practical.

MOVE IN LATER

To make use of the PPR exemption it is not necessary to move in as soon as the property is bought. This can be done at any time (it should be noted, however, that if this occurs more than two years after the purchase the Revenue does not have to agree with your election of this property as your main residence). The last three years will then be free of CGT, even if the property was let for some of this time.

There is no specific time that you must reside in the property before selling it, but a few points are worth noting:

1. A very short time (eg less than six months) might raise Revenue eyebrows.

2. If you do this several times you could find yourself the subject of an Inland Revenue enquiry. They might argue that you never really intended to live in any of the properties on a permanent basis and that you are, in effect, trading or dealing in properties. If they were to take this view they might change your tax structure altogether – taxing profits as *income*, not as capital gain. You would lose both the CGT allowance and the very favourable CGT rate of 18%.

FORM A LIMITED COMPANY?

Forming a limited company radically changes the tax position for the property investor. But it is by no means clear that it will always be for the best. Consider the following:

1. Limited companies do not have an annual CGT allowance (see above) to set against the gain.

2. The CGT rate of 18% compares favourably with the minimum corporation tax rate of 20% (rising to 22% from 1 April 2009)

3. In addition to the corporation tax payable there may be further income tax to pay if profits are distributed as income instead of being retained in the company.

4. If you already own properties and transfer them into a limited company you will be liable for CGT on any gain from the time they were bought. The transfer must be made at the market value.

5. An accountant is essential and company accounts are a costly annual outlay.

It is essential to take professional advice before considering this route.

Income Tax

While capital gains tax (CGT) can come as a nasty and painful surprise, it is, in the end, a one-off nasty and painful surprise. Income tax, on the other hand, is an annual attack on rental profits and a permanent source of misery. The tax rates for 07/08 are 10%, 22% and 40% (the non-savings rates) depending on income level. From April 2008 the 10% rate disappears, the basic rate falls to 20% and the higher rate stays at 40%. But it is not all bad news.

Like CGT, income tax can be mitigated in a number of ways by using the standard reliefs and allowances available to everyone who has an income from property.

MORTGAGE INTEREST
By far the most important of these, for most investors, is the interest paid on the mortgage taken out to buy the investment property. In most cases this will be a buy-to-let mortgage (see Chapter 4). Unlike, therefore, the interest paid on a residential mortgage (which attracts no tax relief at all), 100% of an investment mortgage interest is allowable and can be offset against rental income.

There is a further bonus for the investor who raises finance for rental investment on *his own residential home*. So long as the purpose of the mortgage (or remortgage) is to invest in rental property, the interest on this, too, is an allowable expense. This is despite the fact that a residential mortgage does not attract tax relief. Only the amount raised for investment purposes, however, is allowable.

Finally, it should be noted that only the interest on the mortgage is tax deductible. Capital repayments do not qualify for tax relief.

OTHER MORTGAGE COSTS

Some other costs, associated with obtaining the investment mortgage, are also allowable:

- A broker's fee.
- The lender's arrangement fee.

Note, however, that the cost of the valuation required for the purchase is not an allowable expense for income tax purposes. It can, however, be used to mitigate the CGT on resale (see Chapter 28).

REPAIRS AND MAINTENANCE

As might be expected, ongoing repair and maintenance costs can be offset against rental income. If the work prevents the property from deteriorating, the cost is allowable. The costs of maintaining boilers, repairing leaking radiators, patching up the roof, fixing the fence, painting (inside and out), repairing furniture, treating damp, etc. are all allowable expenses. Keep all invoices and receipts.

A distinction, however, needs to be made between these costs and the cost of *improvements*. A new bathroom, for example, is an improvement. A loft conversion is an improvement. These costs can be taken into account on the sale of the property and can mitigate the CGT liability (see Chapter 28) but cannot be used to reduce the tax on rental income. Nor is it possible to claim the notional cost of a repair you won't now have to make because of the new bathroom you have installed!

An exception may be made where the improvement is of such a nature as to bring the property up to acceptable living standards for houses and flats. Double glazing might be considered one such improvement. If in doubt, call the Inland Revenue Helpline (0845 9000 444) and ask. It follows, of course, that what is allowable against income tax cannot be used later to offset CGT.

PRIOR TO LETTING

Unfortunately the Revenue has little sympathy for you here. The cost of getting the property into shape *before* letting is not allowable. However, the cost of advertising is, as are the fees charged by an agent, if you use one.

10% WEAR AND TEAR

This applies to the furniture and furnishings (not the fittings) in furnished rental property. Some 10% of the annual rental income can be claimed to allow for the natural deterioration of the furniture and furnishings.

If, however, you yourself pay certain bills, such as council tax (bills normally paid by the tenant), you must deduct this amount from the rent before you calculate the 10% wear-and-tear allowance.

You can choose instead (not as well!) to claim for the replacement cost of any individual item (e.g. a carpet). Note, however, that it is the replacement cost that must be claimed. If you have sold the old sofa, you will have to deduct the price you got for it from the cost of the new one. This is the replacement cost.

In most cases, using the 10% wear-and-tear allowance is far simpler and a great deal more cost effective.

LEGAL AND PROFESSIONAL FEES
You may decide you need a solicitor to draw up a lease or to take legal action to remove a tenant. These costs are allowable. Similarly, an agent's fees for managing a property and an accountant's fees for drawing up accounts are tax deductible.

SERVICES PROVIDED
You may decide to provide services for your tenants that have a direct cost implication for yourself. These could include, for example, gardening costs or the cost of cleaning or the cost of communal heating. If *you* pay any of these costs, you can set them against rental income, so long as they are wholly and exclusively for the purpose of letting.

ENERGY SAVING ALLOWANCE
Some might say about time too! At last an incentive for landlords to conserve energy. The incentive centres around two forms of heat insulation – loft and cavity wall. The cost of installing these is tax deductible. Each tax year, however, an upper limit is set for the **total** cost allowable for these works in any one building. Check the Inland Revenue Helpline for the current limit.

ONGOING BILLS
By virtue of owning the property (whether it is let or not) the landlord has ongoing bills to pay:

♦ The property must be insured. The cost of buildings and contents cover is allowable. Also allowed is the cost of a rental guarantee policy, designed to compensate the landlord for the loss of rent. If a claim on such a policy has been met, however, the amount received under the claim must be declared as income. The cost of personal policies (such as life and critical illness policies) is not allowable.

♦ If the property is leasehold, there will normally be ground rent to pay to the freeholder. This is tax deductible.

♦ The tenant would normally pay council tax but, if the landlord pays this, the cost is allowable.

♦ If the landlord pays the water rates, the cost is allowable.

OTHER EXPENSES

There will always be other miscellaneous costs. If these are incurred wholly and exclusively in connection with the rental business, they will be allowable. Examples are as follows:

♦ Advertising for tenants.
♦ Travelling (car or public transport).
♦ Stationery and postage.
♦ Telephone calls.
♦ Costs incurred in collecting rent.

Proper records and receipts should be kept.

RENT-A-ROOM EXEMPTION

This scheme is intended to benefit the homeowner who lets out a room in his only or main home. It does not include the following:

- A room let in your holiday home in the west of Ireland!
- A room let as an office.
- A room let in the course of a bed-and-breakfast or guest-house business.
- A room let while you are living abroad.
- A room let in your own home while you occupy accommodation provided by your employer.

It is clear that the scope of the exemption is narrowly drawn, but it is valuable, none the less. If the letting qualifies under the scheme, the rent received is free of tax. All you have to do is tick the appropriate box on your tax return.

As always, there is a limit to the Chancellor's generosity. A cap is placed on the rental income that is free of tax. Rent above this figure is not exempt. The cap is currently £4,250 (this figure is the *gross* rent, i.e. *before* allowing for any expenses). To put this in perspective, a 40% taxpayer would have to earn £7,083.33 to achieve (after tax) the same income. It is subject to change (it was set at this figure in the 1997/8 tax year) and, who knows, might be increased one day. Check the Inland Revenue helpline for the up-to-date figure.

If you receive rent in excess of the limit, you can choose how this excess amount is taxed. There are two options:

- Allow the excess to be taxed without the benefit of any relief for expenses, etc. You can claim nothing for the costs incurred by your lodger.

- ◆ Don't use the rent-a-room exemption at all and add the rent received to other rental income in the normal way, thus making use of all available reliefs.

Always remember you can opt out of the rent-a-room scheme altogether if you have incurred losses as a result of the scheme and wish to offset these losses against other rental income. This should be made clear in your next tax return.

There would normally be no council tax implications as a result of the scheme. But if your tenant happens to be a *full-time student*, there may be benefits for yourself. As full-time students do not pay council tax, you may qualify for a 25% council tax reduction as a result of your new lodger. Contact your local council.

A further, important consideration is the question of CGT on the sale of the property concerned. Despite the income earned from the rent-a-room scheme, there is no CGT liability on the sale of the property. It continues to benefit from full principal private residence exemption.

Finally, a few points to note if there is a mortgage on the property. Strictly speaking, the lender should be informed beforehand and must give permission for the letting. Secondly, a lender will not normally accept the rental income when calculating how much they are prepared to lend on the property.

PERSONAL ALLOWANCE

Lastly, having reduced your taxable rental income by making use of all available reliefs and exemptions, don't forget to apply your personal tax allowance. Each tax year we are given an individual tax allowance which can be set against our income (£5,225 for 07/08). If you have taxable income in addition to rental income, the allowance should be set against the total figure.

Income Tax Manoeuvres

The scope for further mitigation of income tax is limited to the areas of joint ownership compared with sole ownership, and 50/50 ownership compared with a different split. As the level of income tax crucially depends on an individual's overall earnings, it does make a difference if the joint owners of a property have significantly different levels of income.

SOLE PURCHASE

If a property is in sole ownership, the owner alone is taxed on any income generated. If he is already a 40% taxpayer, the rental income will simply be added to his other income and be taxed at 40%. Conversely, a basic-rate or lower-rate taxpayer will have considerably less tax to pay. When two people, one basic or lower rate and one higher, are considering a joint purchase, income tax can be saved by the purchase being made solely in the name of the lower taxpayer.

There are, however, a few caveats:

◆ While there may be savings on income tax, it is a different matter when it comes to capital gains tax (CGT). When the property is sold, there will be only one lot of CGT allowance, instead of two, making for a higher CGT bill.

◆ Switching to joint ownership later can cause financial headaches. If the two people concerned are not married or in a civil partnership, there will be a CGT liability for any gain since the purchase. If there is a mortgage involved there may be a liability to Stamp Duty Land Tax (SDLT).

SWITCH TO SOLE OWNERSHIP

If the property is already jointly owned, it is possible to change to sole ownership. This can, however, have the following consequences:

◆ CGT implications, as above.
◆ SDLT implications, as above.
◆ Considerable outlay in professional fees.
◆ Potential problems with the mortgage lender who may not want responsibility for the mortgage to rest solely on the shoulders of the lower earner.

BUY IN UNEQUAL SHARES

When a property is owned jointly, the Revenue assumes a 50/50 split and automatically levies income tax on this basis. If, however, the property is held in different shares (e.g. 25/75), in order to push most of the income to the lower earner, they will levy income tax in proportion to the actual ownership split.

However, they will only do this if you declare the true position regarding ownership of the property. There is, as might be expected, a special form for this (form 17), called 'Notice of declaration of beneficial interests in joint property and income'. To avail of this facility, certain conditions have to be fulfilled:

◆ You are husband and wife or in a civil partneship, living together.

- You must actually own the property in unequal shares. It is not enough to declare that you do. The Revenue may ask for proof, such as sight of the deeds. You cannot simply elect to be taxed in a proportion that suits you.

- You have a right to the rental income in proportion to your share of the property.

- You now wish to be taxed on the actual basis of your ownership.

- You must return the form within 60 days of signing and dating it. The declaration will then be effective from the date it was signed.

There are certain consequences that follow from making this declaration and these should be carefully considered beforehand. The declaration, once made, cannot be changed again until:

- your interests in the property or income change
- you cease to be a married couple or in a civil partnership living together.

Useful Addresses

LANDLORD ASSOCIATIONS
Residential Landlords' Association (RLA)
1 Roebuck Lane
Sale
Manchester M33 7SY
Tel: 0161 962 0010
Tel: 0845 666 5000
Fax: 0845 665 1845
Web: www.rla.org.uk

National Landlord Association (NLA)
22–26 Albert Embankment
London SE1 7TJ
Tel: 0870 241 0471
Fax: 0871 247 7535
Web: www.landlords.org.uk

LETTING AGENTS' ASSOCIATIONS
The Association of Residential Letting Agents (ARLA)
Maple House
53–55 Woodside Road
Amersham
Bucks HP6 6AA
Tel: 0845 345 5752
Fax: 01494 431 530
Web: www.arla.co.uk

SPECIALIST BUY-TO-LET LENDERS

Birmingham Midshires
PO Box 81
Pendeford Business Park
Wobaston Road
Wolverhampton WV9 5HZ
Tel: 0845 300 2627
Web: www.askbm.co.uk/

Bristol and West
PO Box 27
One temple Quay
Bristol BS99 7AX
Tel: 0845 300 8000
Web: www.bristol-west.co.uk

Mortgage Express Ltd
Customer services
PO Box 4
Bingley BD16 2LW
Tel: 0500 11 11 30
Web: www.mortgage-express.co.uk

Paragon Mortgages Ltd
St Catherine's Court
Herbert Road
Solihull
West Midlands
B91 3QE
Tel: 0800 440 099

Tel: 0800 375 777

Web: www.paragon-mortgages.co.uk

TENANCY DEPOSIT SCHEMES

Tenancy Deposit Solutions Ltd

3rd Floor

Kingmaker House

Station Road

New Barnet

Hertfordshire EN5 1NZ

Tel: 0871 703 0552

Fax: 08456 34 34 03

Web: www.mydeposits.co.uk

The Dispute Service Ltd

PO Box 541

Amersham

Bucks HP6 6ZR

Tel: 0845 226 7837

Fax: 01442 253 193

Web: www.thedisputeservice.co.uk

The Deposit Protection Service

The Pavilions

Bridgwater Road

Bristol BS99 6AA

Tel: 0870 7071 707

Web: www.depositprotection.com

Useful Websites

AUCTION HOUSES
www.ifey.com

FINDING TENANTS
www.accommodationforstudents.com

www.loot.com

www.fish4homes.com

www.gumtree.com

GOVERNMENT INFORMATION
www.odpm.gov.uk

www.publications.parliament.uk

HOUSE PRICE ANALYSIS
www.landreg.gov.uk.

www.houseprices.co.uk

www.myhouseprice.com

www.upmystreet.com

www.hometrack.co.uk

www.nationwide.co.uk/hpi

www.housepricecrash.co.uk

www.ourproperty.co.uk

uk.realestate.yahoo.com

INDEPENDENT FINANCIAL ADVISERS
www.unbiased.co.uk

INLAND REVENUE

inlandrevenue.gov.uk

LEGAL MATTERS

www.landlordlaw.co.uk
www.landlordzone.co.uk
www.hmcourts-service.gov.uk

RENTAL GUARANTEE INSURANCE

www.rentchecks.com
www.homeletuk.com

TENANT CHECKS

www.experian.co.uk
www.equifax.co.uk
www.landlordzone.co.uk
www.ticagroup.com
www.eletsure.com

Index